Struggle and Suffrage in Huddersfield

Struggle and Suffrage in Huddersfield

Women's Lives and the Fight for Equality

Vivien Teasdale

PEN & SWORD HISTORY

AN IMPRINT OF PEN & SWORD BOOKS LTD.
YORKSHIRE – PHILADELPHIA

First published in Great Britain in 2018 by
Pen & Sword HISTORY
An imprint of
Pen & Sword Books Ltd
Yorkshire – Philadelphia

Copyright © Vivien Teasdale, 2018

ISBN 978 1 52671 278 3

The right of Vivien Teasdale to be identified as Author of this work has been asserted by her in accordance with the Copyright, Designs and Patents Act 1988.

A CIP catalogue record for this book is available from the British Library.

All rights reserved. No part of this book may be reproduced or transmitted in any form or by any means, electronic or mechanical including photocopying, recording or by any information storage and retrieval system, without permission from the Publisher in writing.

Printed and bound in England by CPI Group (UK) Ltd, Croydon, CR0 4YY

Pen & Sword Books Limited incorporates the imprints of Atlas, Archaeology, Aviation, Discovery, Family History, Fiction, History, Maritime, Military, Military Classics, Politics, Select, Transport, True Crime, Air World, Frontline Publishing, Leo Cooper, Remember When, Seaforth Publishing, The Praetorian Press, Wharncliffe Local History, Wharncliffe Transport, Wharncliffe True Crime and White Owl.

For a complete list of Pen & Sword titles please contact
PEN & SWORD BOOKS LIMITED
47 Church Street, Barnsley, South Yorkshire, S70 2AS, England
E-mail: enquiries@pen-and-sword.co.uk
Website: www.pen-and-sword.co.uk

Or

PEN AND SWORD BOOKS
1950 Lawrence Rd, Havertown, PA 19083, USA
E-mail: Uspen-and-sword@casematepublishers.com
Website: www.penandswordbooks.com

Contents

Acknowledgements	vii
Introduction	1
Chapter One: Family Life	3
Marriage	3
Maternity and childcare	4
Feeding the family	10
Keeping house	14
Education	19
Changing family patterns	29
Chapter Two: Quality of Life	32
Poverty and the workhouse	34
The Board of Health	38
Medical practitioners	39
Medical care in Huddersfield	41
Treatment of the disabled	43
Pensions	48
Chapter Three: Working Life	51
Domestic service	51
Local businesses	54
Textiles	55
Shop work	56
Office work	58
Trade unions	61
Travel and transport	62
Chapter Four: Political Life	64
Local government	64
Votes for women	65

Chapter Five: Community Life 71
    Women's organisations and the Embryonic Welfare State 71
    Religion 76

Chapter Six: Legal Life 81
    As a criminal 81
    In prison 84
    As law enforcers 87

Chapter Seven: Social Life 92
    Shopping 92
    Fashion 95
    Arts 98
    Sports 104
    Entertainment 108

Chapter Eight: Impact of War 116
    The South African (Boer) War 116
    The First World War 117
    The Second World War 124

Chapter Nine: A Moving Population 133
    Emigration 133
    Immigration 134
    Irish 135
    Jews 136
    Polish 137
    Commonwealth countries 138

Bibliography 139

Endnotes 145

Index 151

Acknowledgements

So many people are involved in the production of a book it's difficult to know where to start when trying to acknowledge their help. My thanks go to the staff at the West Yorkshire Archive Service, Kirklees who are unfailingly helpful in producing research material and suggesting further research, as are the staff at the University of Huddersfield archives. My thanks also to the staff at the local studies library, Huddersfield, for their support.

I very much appreciated the help of Kath Croft, Mr and Mrs Dixon, Eileen Chilvers and Neville Sheard for giving me their time, family stories and photographs, which always enhance any historical account. Dave Pattern (*Huddersfield Exposed*) and David Ford (Huddersfield Industrial Society) gave me permission to use illustrations from their work. Andrew Hirst at the *Huddersfield Examiner* for his help in finding the story of the NSPA and for permission to use the NSPA photograph. Maps appear with acknowledgement to the Ordnance Survey. Other photographs and illustrations are from the author's collection.

The staff at Pen & Sword have been very helpful in answering my queries and providing support through the publishing process.

As always, I rely heavily on the support of friends and family for their encouragement and endless supplies of cups of tea. My thanks to all of them.

Introduction

The years between 1850 and 1950 probably saw greater changes in the lives of women than at any other time in history. Changes in working life, in family life, in legal status and in how they could spend their leisure time all developed and enhanced women's lives. In this they were aided by some men, held back and castigated by others. Many women too did not approve of these changes and opposed the women who agitated for reform. While gaining the franchise was only a part of the changes women demanded, it was probably the most important because when women entered political life it gave them an official voice in the government of the country, in proposing and scrutinising laws that affected them as well as men.

Much of the impact of the changes depended on what part of society you belonged to. Class, as well as gender, affected where you lived, what jobs were available, what, if any, education you received and, particularly for women, how you lived your life and ran the household. The average life expectancy for someone in the upper classes in 1890 was 60 years of age; for the working classes it was 35. Middle-class death rate for babies was four in every hundred. For the working-class, thirty-three in every hundred babies died before their first birthday.

This book is intended as an introduction to a fascinating but very wide-ranging subject, giving an overview of the different areas in which women's lives have been transformed and why they changed, rather than an in-depth study of one or two aspects of the subject. It also acknowledges the huge contribution to those changes wrought by many women in Huddersfield, such as Emily Siddon, Mary Blamires and Mary Sykes. It is hoped this book will point the way to further reading or study, helping to give a broad understanding of how far women's lives have altered and how much they needed to change over the timescale. Many more changes have been enacted since 1950, though there are still inequalities that need to be addressed.

Wage/price comparison

Comparing wages and prices is necessarily difficult because so much depends on finding consistent information. The tables below give an approximate idea of the wages earned for various occupations and what those wages might buy. There would, of course, have been many variations within each category.

Occupation	1850 (per week)	1900 (per week)	1950 (per week)
Labourer	9-12 shillings	15-20 shillings	£4-£5
Skilled worker	22 shillings	38 shillings	£10-£12
Teacher (female)	11 shillings	15-38 shillings	£7-£12

Item	1850	1900	1950
Potatoes, lb	4d	1d	1d
Cheese, lb	4d	5d	12d
Loaf, lb	2d-3d	3d-4d	8d
Beer, pint	4d	9d	1 shilling
Rent, week	4d	10-12 shillings	20 shillings

CHAPTER ONE

Family Life

Marriage

The Victorians defined a woman's 'sphere of influence' as being domestic, while a man's was 'public'. By 1850, many men could vote, they could enter any job for which they were fit by education, background or wealth. They could own property and sue in the courts for any damage to their property. On marriage, they became the legal owners of their wives and any income or possessions they had. They could beat them, rape them, lock them up and take away their children.

In 1857, Parliament passed the Matrimonial Causes Act, which established civil courts for divorce and made it easier for ordinary people to obtain divorce or separation. Men could divorce simply because of adultery by their wife. Women had to prove adultery and another offence such as cruelty or desertion by their husband.

Divorce was still beyond the hopes of most of the working-class, but they could ask for separation and protection of property orders. Lydia Singleton of Armitage Bridge married in 1853, but her husband deserted her. She worked as a milliner, eventually earning sufficient to own some property. In 1867, her husband suddenly returned wanting her to live with him again. Under the 1857 Act, she was able to apply for protection for her property and earnings.[1]

Women were still not considered fully able to deal with their own lives, though. When Emma Senior was 16, she became suicidal and tried to cut her throat. In 1868, she married Joshua Messenger, but then took Joshua to court on a charge of cruelty. The case was dismissed since she was considered to be 'insane' because of her attempted suicide eleven years previously.

In 1871, she was sent to the West Riding Pauper Lunatic Asylum where a report states that 'her husband has not treated her well and it is suspected that she has not had enough to eat'. She was discharged in October, but readmitted about six weeks after she had given birth to her second daughter, Jane. She was very violent and dangerous to herself and to others, so had to be restrained.

When Emma underwent a physical examination the doctors were shocked to find that she was 'dreadfully bruised' with large discolorations on both arms and shoulders, and her chest, some inflicted with a stick or strap. One of her lower ribs was fractured and she had problems breathing.

The doctors and guardians did not let the matter rest. Her husband was charged with brutally assaulting her, and prosecuted by the police on the instructions of the Commissioners in Lunacy. The magistrates believed the guardians, where they had previously not believed Emma's pleas and now decided that undue force had been used, committing Joseph to prison for two months. Emma did not appear in court and may not have even been aware that her husband had been prosecuted on her behalf[2].

Emma was back in the asylum in December 1872, again shortly after giving birth to another child, Joe. She did not have any particular treatment at the asylum, was just fed, rested and given a little labour in the laundry. She was discharged in December 1873, having been there for twelve months. Unfortunately, there was nowhere else for her to go except home to her husband and family.[3]

Maternity and childcare

Few, other than medical staff, understood how bodies worked, thus, diagnosing pregnancy would often not happen until quite a late stage – some young women didn't even realise they were pregnant until they actually gave birth. Antenatal care was, therefore, almost non-existent. Expectant women were often anaemic, undernourished and overworked. While the wealthy would be cosseted and could afford to see a doctor, those lower down the scale relied on other women in the family, neighbours and local 'gossips' to act as midwives – who also laid out the bodies if things went wrong. Two major causes of death in childbirth were puerperal fever, a bacterial infection appearing soon after giving birth, and haemorrhage.

When Mary Ann Brook of Moldgreen went into labour, she called the local midwife, Nancy Bedford. Nancy was well-known in the area, having a 'practice' of over thirty families. A baby boy was born, but Mary had massive bleeding and the surgeon was called for. Despite his efforts, Mary died.[4]

If the baby survived the birth, childcare would be needed, perhaps even more so if the mother died. Wealthy women had the luxury of staying in bed for a number of weeks after a birth, many working-class women returned to work. The Factory Act of 1892 prohibited the employment of women for a month after giving birth. Many working-class women would not have been able to survive that long without a wage, so probably returned anyway. The midwife, and doctor if he'd been called, had to be paid for.

Some women took in a number of children as 'baby farmers'. There were no controls on women setting up any kind of baby care business until the 1890 Infant Life Protection Act, when baby minders had to register with the local authority, but this was often flouted.

In 1900, Emma Ford, a domestic servant, answered an advertisement in a Leeds paper. Mrs May Duckham wished to adopt a child. Emma had an illegitimate child, Arthur, who was looked after by Emily Copeland but Emma took the opportunity to unburden herself of the 5 shillings (25p) weekly childcare fees. She met May Duckham who said she was the wife of a doctor from Kent and wished to adopt the baby. Emma borrowed the £20 premium from her employer and handed over little Arthur.

May Duckham toured the country taking children for money. The courts found evidence of at least nine children, four of whom had died, though it could not be proved exactly how. The rest were found abandoned with other women or in a workhouse. May Duckham was charged with obtaining money under false pretences and sentenced to nine months in Wakefield Prison. Young Arthur survived and was back with Emily Copeland in 1901, listed as her adopted son.[5]

It was 1926 before the adoption process became the subject of any formal law. By 1949, more stringent laws ensured compulsory registration for child minders and the adoption process was tightened up.

Dealing with the illegitimate child

There were a number of ways in which an unwanted pregnancy could be dealt with. If the family gave some sort of support, the girl might be sent away to stay with friends, other family members or, if they had the money, to stay in lodgings near a 'Magdalen' hospital or mother and baby home until the baby was born. It could then be sent for adoption, either to complete unknowns, in which case they would probably never meet again, or to family members who lived further away and the baby could be passed off as a cousin. Sometimes, the grandmother would bring up the child as her own.

A second solution would be to try to abort the baby. Many women knew something of herbal medicine and many of the patent medicines advertised as help for 'women's troubles' would work as abortifacients. The girl could also be taken to a back-street abortionist, despite the risks.

If the father was known, the girl could try to obtain maintenance for the child. When Alice Firth accompanied her doctor, James Webb Booth, to his surgery for treatment for her toothache, he raped her. She didn't report the rape, feeling she wouldn't be believed, but Booth gave her money to go away to her brother's house, then reneged on his promise to send more money and denied he was the father. The court thought otherwise and imposed a 5-shillings-per-week (25p) maintenance order on him.[6]

A final solution to the problem of illegitimate children was to give no support to the mother whatsoever. The girl was then likely to end up on the streets or in the workhouse. Another way a child might end up in the workhouse was through the behaviour of its mother. Sarah Ratcliffe lived with an old man called Joseph Spencer at Storthes, Moldgreen. She was known to be cruel to the child and neglected it. He was so worried he complained to the police and Sarah ended up in court. She was sentenced to three months in prison and the child was handed over to the care of the parish authorities.[7]

A common place to dispose of babies' bodies was the 'petty' or toilet. In amongst the ashes it was quite likely to be missed and, once emptied into the night-soil cart, it was impossible to be sure who had put it there. Women who survived the birth but concealed the baby might find themselves in prison for a few months, but the courts were sometimes quite lenient. Proving that the baby had been alive at birth was almost impossible, as was proving that the mother had deliberately concealed it and not simply abandoned it.

There were peaks of illegitimacy during wars. The father might have been a member of a foreign military billeted in England, such as the American and Canadian soldiers in the Second World War. Some did marry the girl – there were more than 60,000 'war brides' who left England to go to America after the Second World War, but many men simply disappeared back to their barracks and the USA, never to be seen again.

In 1918, the National Council for the Unmarried Mother and her Child was set-up to help the women and to reform the various laws that discriminated against them. The group set-up hostels as an alternative to the workhouse. The council is now known as Gingerbread.

In 1925, for the first time, National Insurance payments were given to married women who were destitute, but nothing could be claimed by divorced or single mothers. It was 1948 before the benefit was finally given to all mothers in need.

Family planning

Family planning was barred by the church, but the feminist movements saw birth control as necessary for women – it should be their choice how many children to have. The better-off were able to avoid some pregnancies, either by abstinence or the use of rubber sheaths, but for working-class women the continual cycle of pregnancies affected their health and, consequently, the health of their babies.[8] The Co-operative Women's Guild collected letters from working-class women that included examples of a woman married at 19 having eleven children and one miscarriage in twenty years. Another had five children and one miscarriage in nine years. As these were poorer women, they would probably have been working at least part-time or at home during these pregnancies as well as doing heavy housework.

Abortion could be induced by taking hot baths, or drinking gin or rat poison, or using implements such as sticks or knitting needles, or taking medicine 'for women's troubles', which assured that they would 'remove obstructions and irregularities', often containing abortifacient ingredients.

Margaret Dearnley and Mary Haigh were accused of conspiring to murder Hannah Littlewood by using 'certain instruments for the purpose of procuring abortion'. The case was heard at Leeds Assizes but 'before the charges were gone into the Ladies Gallery, which was crowded, was cleared'. No explanation was given for this, but it was probably because the subject matter would be considered too delicate for female ears.[9]

According to Hannah's husband, she'd never had a miscarriage before. Hannah had called on her friend, Mary Haigh, and they both went to Margaret Dearnley's house in Commercial Square. Margaret and Hannah went away for a while, then Mary and Hannah went to the theatre. The next day Hannah was taken fatally ill. John admitted that their neighbour, Elizabeth Sykes, had given her pennyroyal tea when she was taken ill and he'd given her a strong dose of salts. The doctors who carried out the post-mortem agreed that death was from septicaemia or blood poisoning caused by abortion. They found an internal scar that could have been caused by a piece of wood called a slubber's brooch, used for abortions. Had it not been for that scar, the evidence suggested natural abortion. Hannah had also developed pneumonia soon after her visit to Mrs Dearnley's. A slubber's brooch was found under Dearnley's bed. Also a knitting needle and a crochet hook, both of which could have been used in an abortion.

The jury found Margaret guilty of procuring abortion, but not guilty of murder. She was sentenced to ten years in prison.

The Infant Life Preservation Act of 1926 reaffirmed the illegality of abortion in any form except when needed to save the life of the mother and performed by a doctor.

In 1918, the Maternity and Child Welfare Act allowed, but didn't compel, local councils to set-up maternity homes, infant welfare centres, crèches, and to provide paid midwives and health visitors as well as milk and food for mothers and children. They were still not allowed to offer contraceptive advice.

It was 1921 before the first English birth control clinic, strictly for married women, was opened in London by Marie Stopes. The Women's Co-operative Guild, at their 1923 conference, called on the Ministry of Health to alter regulations prohibiting the dissemination of birth control information at public clinics. But it was six years later before the Ministry of Health allowed, but again did not force, local health authorities to provide birth control advice for married women 'for whom a further pregnancy would be detrimental to health'.

In 1948, Huddersfield Council discussed the setting up of a birth control clinic. Reassurance was given that Dr Stang, who had agreed to run the clinic, would only give advice, when necessary, to married women where pregnancy, in her opinion, was inadvisable. The council stressed that it would see the information was not given 'carelessly' and that no one would receive it 'who should not do so', i.e. unmarried women.[10]

The various clinics eventually came together under one body which, in 1939, became the Family Planning Association.

Feeding the family

In the home

Housing and feeding the family took up most of the family budget for the working classes. The staple diet was of bread, potatoes, onions and some meat, including sweetbreads (part of the thymus gland and pancreas), beast cheek, brains, heart and pluck (lungs and intestines, usually of sheep) together with chitterlings (pig or sheep intestines, cooked or sometimes stuffed), black pudding and haslet (stale bread mixed with minced pork and sage). Kippers and cheese were cheap meals and cups of tea became the principal drink along with beer.

Many families didn't have any cooking facilities. In some houses or rented rooms there might not even be a fire on which food could be cooked. Meals were therefore either cold or warm pies bought from street sellers. When Alice Flynn moved to Lindley, the house had only one room downstairs with a tap but no wash basin. Water was run off into a pan, to heat up on an open range.[11]

Those earning over £100 a year could afford a good diet, including a range of meats, plenty of vegetables and fish. Fresh food, brought to towns on the railways, gradually became available to all, except the very poorest.

Kedgeree was very popular as a breakfast food, though the original spiced rice and lentil mixture of India was soon changed in England by adding smoked fish and hard-boiled eggs. Between 1850 and 1950, people began to use more processed food. Tinned, bottled, powdered and dried foods became available.

By the 1940s, most homes in towns had electricity so were able to use electric kettles, fridges, and cookers, but only the wealthiest could afford to buy these until well after the Second World War so food had to be bought little and often. Mrs Beeton's cookery books listed the foods that should be available each month to help cooks plan their meals.[12]

Outside the home

Workers had a packed lunch of bread with cheese, or a pasty and cold tea. They could buy a pie or, in the mills, take an onion or bacon to cook on shovels in the furnaces. There were rarely any rooms provided in which to eat and no canteens until the twentieth century.

Eating out for the wealthy was primarily social. For the middle classes it was small groups or lunch at work. For the working classes it was street food or a packed lunch. With changes in transport, more people lived in the suburbs. Women came to town either for work, shopping or socialising. Department stores realised that by providing tearooms selling snacks, cakes, scones or crumpets and a drink, they could attract more customers, particularly women. The Co-operative Stores opened a tearoom on John Street in 1892 and another on Buxton Road in 1903. This was much larger with a reading room and smoking room.

Smaller businesses had tearooms within their shop. Mrs Briggs, described in 1871 as an 'ornamental confectioner', produced wedding and other cakes, sold tinned goods and ran a refreshment room offering tea, wine and chops. The business was large enough to need three confectioners, two assistants and three apprentices. Street sellers provided hot chestnuts, baked potatoes, pea soup, pigs' trotters, pies, gingerbread and muffins.

Many institutions and charities held lectures and provided information about the institution and entertainments. They also included 'trays' or teas, provided and served by a ladies' committee that supported the organisation. Sandwiches, cakes and tea were available, sometimes catering for hundreds of people. The event usually ended with a round of thanks, including to 'the ladies', which was often the only hint that women were present at the meetings.

A decade later, bank holidays gave people the chance to have a day away. Different foods could be tried such as potted shrimps from Morecambe Bay or oysters. More people were taking longer holidays, too. The Co-op dividend could be saved up to pay for a holiday. Friendly societies organised trips away.

Cookery books such as Mrs Beeton's *The Book of Household Management* of 1861 and Mrs A.B. Marshall's *Book of Cookery* of 1888 became popular. Marguerite Patten was one of the first television cooks, when she demonstrated cooking on limited resources during the Second World War.

Advice was given on economy and just about everything else in the early cook books. Mrs Beeton provided recipes for 'Plain Family Dinners' and included 'using up' advice. After a full Sunday dinner, 'the remains of turbot warmed in oyster sauce' is recommended on Monday, together with cold pork from the weekend's roast.

Adulteration of foods

Women were expected to keep their households healthy but had no idea what was in the food they were buying. Milk could have water added to it to make it go further, chalk to make it look whiter, or red pigment to give it an added creamy colour. The worst additive was Boracic acid, used to purify and remove any sour taste or smell when it had gone off. Unfortunately, Boracic acid concealed the presence of bovine tuberculosis (TB). Milk was drunk raw, not pasteurised. Eventually, the link between raw milk and TB was realised and by the mid-1920s, large amounts of milk were pasteurised.

Butter, gin, pickles, wine and preserves all might have copper added to improve their colour. Vinegar was adulterated with sulphuric acid. Sweets might contain red lead or mercury to give a nice red colour. Green could come from copper arsenite, blue from Prussian blue or blue vitriol, yellow from gamboge, which was a high irritant, and white from chalk, Cornish clay or even white lead.

Beer or Porter, a kind of stout, might contain small amounts of Nux vomica (strychnine tree), Vitriol (sulphuric acid), Quassia (pesticide) to give it that sharpness that customers expected, or opium to induce the soporific effect of alcohol. Lead might also be added to wine or cider.

Bread could have bean flour, chalk or plaster of Paris added, or alum, which did make it look whiter but is aluminium-based.

There were a number of prosecutions in West Yorkshire for this, though it was admitted that millers were the largest market for alum so it was difficult to find any bread that was not adulterated.[13]

All these adulterants were put in deliberately. Standards of hygiene were low so food and drink might also be contaminated with lice, fleas, straw, hair, and bacteria such as streptococcus.

For toothache, constipation, childbirth pains, parasitic infestation and tuberculosis, a 'Blue pill' would relieve the symptoms. It contained mercury. Syrup of Squill was used for bronchitis and whooping cough, but it also induced vomiting and was an abortifacient. Spirit of sweet nitre was a diuretic and antispasmodic, which nowadays is clearly labelled 'For External Use Only'. Scammony and Jalap were purgatives, given to ease constipation.[14] Both are now considered too strong. 'Grey powder' was a purgative containing mercury, while antimony is a poison used for the same purpose. The Victorians were very keen on having open bowels. This opinion continued into the twentieth century, but the remedies changed to castor oil and cascara.

Some remedies were genuinely merely herbal, such as Whelpton's Purifying Pills, which remained popular into the twentieth century.

If all else failed, laudanum (from opium) could be added to almost anything, including a baby's bottle of milk, or taken by itself. Laudanum was easy to obtain. When Harriet Saunders arrived in Huddersfield, alone, penniless and with nowhere to go, she tried to use laudanum to commit suicide in the railway station rest room. A railway employee found her and sent for the doctor who administered an emetic. Harriet remained ill for several days and was sent to the workhouse to recover before being returned to her original address in Manchester. Surprisingly, she doesn't seem to have been prosecuted for attempted suicide.[15]

Keeping house

Fashionable houses in suburbs such as Edgerton were set in their own grounds. Most of the family had their own room, with attics for the servants, schoolrooms for the children and billiards rooms for entertainment. The family used the drawing room, dining room and library but rarely ventured down to the kitchen and other working rooms. Wealthy women told the housekeeper what was required, but it was the housekeeper's job to ensure the house ran smoothly. However, these houses were not that prevalent and became more rare as the twentieth century progressed.

Middle-class houses had an entrance way, with a front parlour, which would be kept for best and for special visitors. The living room was where the family lived and ate, plus a kitchen and scullery where at least one servant would be responsible for all the cooking and laundry. The servant had an attic room. The children rarely had their own bedroom, though the sexes would be separated. There might be a garden or yard at the back and possibly at the front too. The ladies in these households had to learn to run the house themselves, though they employed one or two servants to do the heavy work.

For the better-off working-class the front door opened straight from the street into the living room. At the back was the kitchen where the family generally congregated and ate. Linoleum and home-made rugs covered the floor. Tables and chairs would be the only furniture, though many saved hard to buy a piano too. There was usually a small scullery with a sink and a copper for laundry. The house could be a back-to-back or could have a small backyard. They may have their own toilet, which would be outdoors, or an outdoor toilet that was shared. Housework was done by the women, sometimes after a full day's work elsewhere, though they may have had daily or weekly help with the heavier jobs.

The poorest housing was much worse, badly built without any suitable roadway or even, during the 1850s, proper toilets. Cooking and heating were poorly provided for or non-existent, nor did they have running water, only a shared tap outside in the yard. There were no servants, the housewife did all the work. In fact, many went out to act as daily domestic servants in better houses.

Some employers built rows of terraced houses for their employees which, generally, were of reasonable quality. Unfortunately, these went with the job so loss of job meant loss of home.

Any washing, of clothes, utensils or body, required the hauling and heating of water. Washing was invariably done on a Monday. Clothes were put in buckets and agitated with a 'posser' or stick to loosen the dirt, then scrubbed with soap before rinsing, put through the mangle to squeeze out as much water as possible, then hung out to dry in communal yards or across streets. Monday or Tuesday evenings would be used to complete the ironing. A wooden clothes horse was put around the open fire for garments to air on. Even curtains needed washing frequently because of the smoke from fires and mill chimneys. Fabrics had to be soaked in salted water to bring the coal dust out before washing too.

Mats were taken out and beaten to dislodge dirt, then shaken. Oven and fire ranges were 'black-leaded' with a paste generally made of ground graphite, lampblack, turpentine and oil. The oven was sometimes washed out with a vinegar mixture. Fires often had brass surrounds that needed polishing. In 'better' households, every day would consist of 'turning out' at least one room, from top to bottom. The most important job was to sweep and scrub the doorstep, then finish with a 'donkey' stone to leave the surface white. This demonstrated to the neighbourhood that you were a good housewife and kept a clean house.

Keeping food fresh was difficult and, in some houses, almost impossible. Even better houses were infested with vermin of various kinds: rats, mice, cockroaches, beetles or silverfish. Cockroaches required plaster of Paris while quicklime dropped into an ants' nest, washed down with boiling water, would sort them out. Bedbugs needed naphtha (derived from petrol and highly flammable), which was painted on the bedhead or onto the mattress.[16]

Shopping had to be done almost daily. Shops sold items in smaller personally wrapped amounts and there were more specialist shops, such as tripe-dressers, milliners, confectioners and lard-makers. Dried fruit, flour, biscuits and tea were weighed out and put into paper bags. Eggs were seasonal products. Hens stop laying in winter under normal conditions, so eggs were preserved in isinglass or liquid paraffin, then used for cooking or baking. Hard-boiled eggs were pickled. Part of the housewife's chores was to preserve food. Hedgerow fruits such as blackberries, elderberries or elderflowers, rosehips and bilberries could be made into jams, drinks or medicines.

Women were also, generally, responsible for paying the day-to-day expenses out of the small amount their husbands may give them. For many women, especially if single or widowed, once rent had been paid there was very little left for food. Shopkeepers may have given credit, at great risk to themselves since the debt may not be paid back. An alternative for many was the pawnbroker. Almost any item could be pawned: shoes, shirts, handkerchiefs, sheets. These would be pawned on a Monday to gain a little money to last the week, and redeemed on Friday, after payday, for the weekend.

The Singleton family[17]

Sarah Singleton was born in 1836 into a fairly well-off, lower-middle-class family. Much against her parents' wishes, in 1855 at the age of 19 she married Thomas Shaw and went to live at Scape. Gone was her comfortable lifestyle, replaced by a very old two-up, one-down cottage with no water except that fetched from the well. No toilet, nothing.

Within ten years she had five boys. There was a gap then, which suggests that she possibly had a number of miscarriages, but in 1870 her daughter Martha was born. Sarah decided she'd had enough and went home to her parents. Taking the children, she walked from Scape to Kirkburton, approximately 10 miles.

Despite having walked that far, her parents refused to let her stay. They fed her and the children and then bought the rail ticket for them to go home, cutting all future contact with her. She had married beneath her and they wanted no more to do with any of them.

Her next child was born in 1871, followed by another boy in 1873. Martha, the only daughter, was always expected to help with the household chores for the whole family, despite the fact that she worked in the local mill as a feeder as well. Then she met John Edward Singleton (no relation to her maternal Singletons), but her father refused permission to marry because she was needed at home, so Martha had to wait until she was 21 before she could leave her father's house and marry John.

Martha and her husband saved up and bought a house in Longwood, later going to live in Milnsbridge. All their five girls went into the mill, but as the family became a little wealthier, the youngest one, Renée, was able to have music lessons, gaining the chance to study at Manchester. Her father refused to let her go, insisting she had to earn a living. She did, however, become a peripatetic music teacher for the local schools in the 1950s.

Another sister, Marion, was a little sickly but very bright. She went to Longwood Grammar School and proved to be a good artist. When she was 13 years of age, she was told she had to leave school and work in the mill, just as her older sisters had done. Despite her teacher pleading for her to remain in school, her father was adamant. The mill was far too noisy for such a fragile child, so she eventually stayed at home as a companion to her mother, never painting, never studying again.

Ada Ann Frobisher[18]

Ada Ann Frobisher, née Sykes, married Fretchfield Frobisher in 1892. Fretch was a pork butcher, eventually setting up his own shop. They had six children. Fretch's diary gives some idea of the family's life.

In 1898, he helped Ada mangle the sheets dry, because they had no servant. They went nettle-picking, partly for food, partly to make nettle beer. They ate tripe, usually in an onion sauce. Heart and pigs' trotters were cooked and eaten, or a calf's head could be made into potted meat. As the wife of a pork butcher, Ada had no shortage of meat for the family.

Rats were frequently mentioned as being a nuisance. There were comments such as: 'Heard a swarm of rats in Kemp's shop.' [next-door] On 7 March 1907: 'Sat in at night with the nasty stench which arises in the back sitting room from the fat brought from Kemp's by the rats under the floorboards.' On 21 April: 'When we got back at 10.30 found Lizzie [the maid] and boys up, frightened by the noise of rats.'

Ada didn't just have her own family to worry about. As they became a little better off, they employed a maid. One, Emma, caused problems when Ada 'found a lot of lice on her [the maid's] pillow. Ada had to wash the girl's head but 'found she could not comb it out as it was quite matted'.

Gas lighting was the norm, with gas for heating and cooking, but by 1900 electricity was being installed in shops and houses. Ada went with her friend, Mrs Lees, to Huddersfield to the "Mains" cookery exhibition, specifically designed to teach women how to cook with the new electric equipment.

As the family moved up the income scale, they bought a motorbike and sidecar. During the First World War Ada was taken 't'look at the wreckage after last Monday's explosion'. This was an explosion at the munitions factory at Low Moor, Bradford where many were killed. The bike was used for holidays too. Often Ada and the youngest child would go on the train, with her husband and the older children following on the motorbike and sidecar or, later, in their car. Holidays included Scarborough and Blackpool, where they would stay in lodgings. In later years they went further afield to Rhyl and to the Isle of Man, which entailed a train to Liverpool and a steamer to Douglas. Ada and her husband sometimes went off for a run by themselves. On one such trip they went to the Lake District, up to Hexham and home via Harrogate and Leeds, all on one day.

In 1906, the diary entry reads: 'Ada and her mother went up to Huddersfield to hear the suffragettes who are in the town speaking for candidates in the bye-election caused by the promotion of Sir James Woodhead to be Railway Commissioner.' By 1912, Ada was canvassing, which caused some irritation with her in-laws. Fretch wrote: 'Aunt came down and asked Hubert at the door where his mother was and he told her quite candidly that she was gone with Mrs Harry Rowbottom, canvassing. I heard her say it was a pity she had nothing else to do.' He obviously had no problem with his wife becoming involved in this way.

His daughters, however, were a different matter. They were kept under strict control. Elsie, the eldest, was 17 on 18 July 1916. She was seen walking with a boy and her father 'had a bit of a talk with her when she got home'. On 4 February 1917: 'Elsie not in when we got home and did not come in until 10, then grieved to hear she had been with that young Sykes again, told her to stop it.'

Elsie never married, though she did go on to teach embroidery well beyond retirement age at the Huddersfield Technical College. The two younger girls, Kathleen and Gladys, went to Greenhead College and became teachers.

Education

The teachers

In Huddersfield in 1861 there were only eighty-two people giving their occupation as teacher. Of these, fifty-six were female. Many of the women were music teachers, suggesting that they were middle-class women needing to earn a living. The majority were single or widowed ladies, often living with daughters who also taught as part of the school.

In 1846, the pupil-teacher scheme was introduced. Children over the age of 13 who showed the right attitude, aptitude and rectitude could be apprenticed for five years to the head teacher. The pupil-teachers studied for an hour before and after school, as well as completing their school lessons during the day. They took an examination annually, which they had to pass in order to continue their training. Girls were paid £7 per annum during training, boys received £10.

At the end of this training, the youngsters received a certificate that qualified them to take a further examination to gain a Queen's Scholarship. They could then go to training college, where the girls received a grant of £20 per annum. After this, they would be certificated teachers. Those not receiving the full training could be employed as uncertificated teachers, at lower pay.

This system enabled many working-class girls to become teachers. Women's colleges were cheaper to run. Women obtained jobs after training because they were cheaper to employ. By the end of the century there were more girls' schools so more teachers were needed.

After the 1870 Elementary Education Act, the numbers of certificated teachers trebled and pupil-teacher numbers doubled. The number of uncertificated teachers, known as assistant teachers, also increased, leading to concerns about the quality of the teaching. Pupil-teacher centres developed to rectify this, with day training colleges linked to universities.

By 1871, the number of teachers in Huddersfield had increased slightly to 110, of whom seventy-five were women. Elizabeth Shepherd and her sister Emily ran a school, though they were only 24 and 17 respectively. Two days a week they employed Madame Tonnelier to teach singing, as well.[19]

The 1891 census shows the changes wrought by the 1870 Education Act. There were almost 600 teachers in Huddersfield, of whom seventy-five per cent were female. Of these, twenty per cent came from somewhere other than Huddersfield, including three born in America and one in Australia. There were fewer private schools or teachers of music.

During both world wars there was a shortage of teachers. Retired female teachers were asked to return to work for the duration of the war. At Longley School, one pupil remembered that the teachers at that time were all women. Miss Jessop, who taught science, seemed very old and kept nodding off during lessons. Miss Brook was a communist and spent one term teaching the children about communism in Russia. Miss Clare taught French and was the fussy, kind type. There were no games for the children as the school sports fields had been turned over to vegetables (which the children had to tend) because of the government's 'Dig for Victory' campaign.[20]

After the 1914-18 war, more money was put into teaching. The marriage bar applied to women teachers so many chose to stay single and independent rather than marry and have to resign. Training, after the 1939-45 war, involved a special training scheme for all who had served at least one year in HM forces or in a war industry. This included training for one year followed by two years' probation. All uncertificated teachers had to train to become certificated, as the profession became for qualified teachers only.

The 1944 Education Act ended the traditional all-age elementary school from 5 to 14, at which point most children left. The new system consisted of primary school from 5 to 11, then secondary school from 11 to 15. The eleven-plus exam was introduced and secondary schools became open to all girls, no matter what their background, enabling many to go on to higher education.

Sheila Dixon[21]

Sheila Dixon went to Whitley Council School in the 1930s. All classrooms had mixed ages in them, at least two 'standards' being in the same classroom with just one teacher. The only heating was a fireplace with a mesh fireguard round it.

There were separate cloakrooms and playgrounds for boys and girls with a low wall between. When it was a nice day, they could go out to play cricket or rounders on the fields behind the New Inn. At Whitley School, children stayed through to age 14 unless they passed the eleven-plus, and then the girls would go to Greenhead High School, which Sheila did. The attitude at Greenhead, especially that of Miss Hill, the head teacher, was that the girls would go into the professions. Her parents agreed for her to go to Derby Teacher Training College for two years to get a teaching certificate. The council paid for the fees and a grant for board. She went on to take a teaching degree at Huddersfield Polytechnic.

Teaching associations

The Church Schoolmasters and Schoolmistresses Benevolent Association was formed to help Church of England teachers, giving financial support and training. By 1869, they had a small branch in Huddersfield. The committee members were Miss J. Smith and Miss H. Stephens, both from Oakes Board School, Miss A. and Miss L. Wilson, Miss Wilcox, Miss Gilliard, Miss Carter and Miss Booth. At one meeting the committee discussed allocating twenty-four annuities between sixty-eight applications and six orphan allowances between twenty-three applications. Not surprisingly, the other main item for discussion was how to raise sufficient funds.[22] The association still exists today.

Teaching was one of the earliest 'white-collar' areas in which women began to take a role in trade unionism. After the 1870 Education Act, many teachers became employees of their local school board and joined together in teaching associations. Huddersfield & District Teachers' Association was formed around 1872, with over seventy members, both male and female. The association put on lectures on such diverse subjects as drawing and natural history to help their members keep up-to-date with their education. All the officers were men, but the committee included Miss Cooper of Seed Hill, Miss Brook of Northgate, Miss Kelly of St Johns, Miss Horton of Seed Hill, Miss Beddows of St Thomas's and Mrs Gaunt of Hillhouse Congregational School.

Membership of the association included National, Wesleyan, British, and School Board school teachers. Teachers in elementary schools, it was said, had so much in common they were able to help one another, but national standards of inspection, teaching and training were needed.[23]

In addition to looking after qualified teachers, a separate Pupil-Teachers Association was formed that ran examinations for the trainees. The managing committee included Mrs Cummins, Miss Livingstone, Miss Byrne, Miss Holmes, Miss Drury and Miss Summerbill. The first three ladies formed part of a delegation to the annual teachers' conference, but only the leading delegates, all men, had their expenses paid. All the representatives to the District Union Committee and to West Yorkshire District Union were men.

To encourage parents to allow their children to study beyond elementary school, many teachers spoke about the benefits of training as a pupil-teacher. Even if they didn't actually go into teaching the extra education and experience helped their entry into the Civil Service, which was seen as a lower-middle-class job to which many aspired.

Over the next few years a new scheme of testing pupil-teachers was introduced, divided into two parts: a) work of pupil-teachers for each year as laid down by the Education Department, and b) syllabus of extra subjects for those pupil-teachers who chose to take them – Latin, French and English languages, maths and music with needlework and domestic economy for the female pupil-teachers.

Some teachers, even the male teachers, recognised the imposition this was for the girls. There was a great deal of emphasis on needlework by the government and, therefore, this took up too much of their curriculum time. Teachers felt that the needlework scheme was utterly impractical and should be withdrawn.

The presentation of three prizes to the three local pupil-teachers who gained the highest marks in the 1879 mid-summer examinations caused some consternation. One of the association's pupil-teachers was Ann Field, who won a five guinea prize (which she also won the following year). The highest pass marks were also won by the girls, which Mr Glendinning said was a warning to the young men 'for school managers would not continue to pay so much higher for male labour than female if they found that the females were able to beat the males in open competition'.

Continuing their studies after initial training to become certificated was easier for boys than girls, who generally had domestic duties at home and often little support from their parents. In 1880 twice as many girls as boys took English literature. Only four girls took music, and only one took Latin. However, ninety-eight girls took domestic economy and fifty-six took needlework. The dilemma for academic girls was that, in order to obtain a job, they usually had to offer domestic subjects, but by taking those as their 'extra' subjects, there was little time left for other academic work.[24]

This affected their careers as it became more difficult for women to gain promotion, and pay was always less. Average salaries for headmasters ranged from £185 to £210. Those for headmistresses from only £80 to £100. For assistant masters, the range was £70 to £80. For assistant mistresses, there were more grades to work through, going from £52 to £60.

The schools

Early schooling was an *ad hoc* affair as many children were too busy working. As laws were introduced to prevent young children being employed, more schools sprang up, though there was no specific school leaving age. The 1870 Education Act ensured access to education for all. Fees were charged but the school board could fund free schools for the poor if ratepayers agreed. In 1880, education became compulsory for all 5- to 12-year olds. If they reached the required standard, they could then go to work. Otherwise they stayed until age 13.

As industrialisation spread, it was realised that workers needed education to become effective employees, leading to the establishment of Mechanics' Institutes (MIs). In Huddersfield, the MI was formed in 1844, followed, surprisingly, by the Female Educational Institute (FEI) in 1846.[25] This appears to be one of the first such institutes, specifically for girls, in the country. It was not, of course, free so only those who could afford to pay the subscription could attend. The fee was 3d (just over 1p) per week, but supporters who made donations to the institute could nominate a pupil to receive their education for just 1d (about a third of a penny). Messrs Lockwood & Keighley paid 2d (just less than 1p) for each of its women workers (who had to pay the remaining 1d) to attend the institute. In speeches at the annual meeting of the FEI there was a plea for more employers to do the same:

> *For there are hundreds of young girls and women in the neighbourhood who, by reason of the early demand of juvenile labour and pecuniary domestic wants, are too often prematurely removed from the day schools.*[26]

The institute provided a basic education, though the minute book of 1856 stated that not enough time was spent on arithmetic and too much on writing. Introducing 'the conditions of health and domestic economy' was suggested, and sewing was one of the largest classes taught. The emphasis was still on women as homemakers.

At the 1858 annual meeting, the chairman commented that the girls were constantly liable to have their studies interfered with, generally by duties at home, and were therefore unable to study continuously, so they found it difficult to reach the attainment of the boys at the MI. This sounded very sympathetic, but then he explained why women should be educated. 'The purpose of teaching arithmetic was to make the young women good managers of families,' he said. It 'must be borne in mind that it was necessary to educate women for the social duties which devolved on them'. He felt that the FEI should have cookery classes and lessons on attending the sick, both of which were needed to make the girls better daughters, better wives and better mothers.[27]

Volunteer teachers and committee members were largely women, though it was the men who held the 'officers' positions on the committee and controlled the finances. A sub-committee was formed of two men who were to give publicity about the institute 'among the work people in the various mills, manufactories etc'. This was considered to be in the 'public' arena, so more appropriate for the men. The women were confined to the classroom. When the institute was invited in

1859 to join a Mechanics' Institute procession, the committee resolved that 'our committee being composed chiefly of ladies [we] cannot join the procession as a body but that the gentlemen be requested to attend and represent the Institute'.

Each class was entitled to elect its own representative to the committee. In 1856 these were: Class I Mary Wood, Class K Fanny Goldthorp, Class L Mary Drake and Class M Mrs Pitkethly.

In 1859, the Yorkshire Union of MIs complained about the discrepancy between the number of males and females in the various institutes in the union, i.e. 21,299 male students but only 2,228 females. The Yorkshire Union suggested that other towns besides Huddersfield should have female Institutes too.

Around half the staff at school were paid qualified teachers. The others were volunteers, primarily women. The committee made regular visits to the classrooms to ensure all was well and took an active part in the life of the Institute.

At the annual meeting of 1878, Joseph Lowenthal commented on classes not being as well-attended as at the MI:

> *It had often been a surprise to him why this institute should not be as well attended as the Mechanics Institute. Though it was necessary and very proper that girls should be at home to render help to their mothers ... he felt it was equally important to obtain an education and their mothers should let them come.*

Though a laudable sentiment, it showed a lack of understanding of the situation most women were in. It was, quite frequently, the father who decided that his daughter had sufficient education for her purposes and should therefore leave schooling and go to work.

By 1883, the FEI was in financial difficulties and had to merge with the Huddersfield Mechanics' Institute, which took over their library and their pupils. From then on there were no ladies to represent the women on the ruling committee and no classes specifically for them, except sewing. Reported speeches from annual meetings show that few girls were mentioned in the top range, except drawing. None seem to have been encouraged to take up subjects such as science or vocational subjects such as textiles.[28]

In 1872, the Huddersfield Girls' College was set-up for middle-class girls.[29] This was totally separate to the MI, which was aimed more at the working-class. Though expecting only twenty or thirty pupils to enrol in the new school, it began with over sixty-five pupils. The preparatory school admitted both boys and girls from age 3 to 7. The lower and upper schools were girls only, but had a wide curriculum including French and German. Pupils were entered for the Cambridge University Local Examinations each year. Though the examinations had been established since 1857, it was only in 1868 that they became available to girls. Miss Harriett M. Cheveley became the college's first and only principal.

Though successful for many years, in 1886 the college amalgamated with the boys' college and the collegiate, also for boys. The three institutions became known as the Huddersfield College, with separate boys' and girls' departments. Miss Cheveley remained as head of the girls' department. In 1893, the college was again in financial difficulties and passed into the hands of a liquidator. The 'last official gathering' was in July when the final prizegiving was held, with all the details being published in the *Huddersfield Chronicle*.[30]

The school board bought the college premises and set-up a higher grade school where the curriculum included reading, composition, arithmetic, English, geography, history, French or German, drawing, music, typewriting, physiography, physiology, magnetism and electricity, and drill for all pupils. The boys also studied bookkeeping, Latin, Euclid (geometry), shorthand, workshop practice, chemistry and mechanics, while the girls got the usual mix of needlework, domestic economy, hygiene and cookery. The school was formally opened in December 1894.

Eventually it was decided to have separate schools for boys and girls. The Girls' High School opened with 236 scholars, taught by a staff of nine regular mistresses, three visiting mistresses and two visiting masters. The school went on to be known as Greenhead High School for Girls, now co-educational. The higher grade school later became Huddersfield Art College.

University education

Women were not allowed to attend university until the late nineteenth century. University College, London was one of the first to allow females to attend lectures in the evenings, but this was only by the agreement of each individual lecturer.

In 1869, Girton College for Women was founded near Cambridge University. In 1878, Lady Margaret Hall for Women was opened at Oxford University. These were residential colleges, but caused controversy because they were seen as tempting women away from their natural destiny of wife and mother. None of the early colleges could give degrees, even though the women followed a suitable curriculum and took the same exam as the men. In 1880, three women were finally granted degrees by the University of London. It was 1920 before Oxford began awarding degrees to women and only in 1948 that Cambridge followed suit. Prior to that, many women studied at Oxbridge then transferred to London in order to gain the proper degree from a university.

The British Federation of University Women was founded in 1907 in order to help bring together those who had degrees. A branch in Huddersfield opened in 1924.

A lady who had her own ideas about work was M.A. Smith. She'd had to leave school at 14 in order to earn a living. In 1920, the National Residential College for Women at Hillcroft in Surrey was formed and Miss Smith applied to the Huddersfield Authority for a grant. She received this and a bursary from the college itself, which enabled her to go to the college for one year. As well as lessons the college arranged visits to the Houses of Parliament, museums, art galleries, nursery schools, law courts, factories and the BBC headquarters. As she said:

> *In a college for working women there is none of that detachment from real life that is possible in a training college with students fresh from school. All of us had*

earned our living before entering college and most of us had known more rough ways than smooth.[31]

At the end of the year, Miss Smith returned to her weaving job in a mill. Many other women also returned to their previous jobs, but they had seen something of the world and some took up voluntary work on their return. A few managed to use their new education to improve their working life too.

Changing family patterns

We think of families with stepchildren or generations having to share a house as being something relatively modern, but in previous years they were very common. Widows needed support or women died in childbirth, leaving men needing someone to look after small children. If families grew too large, some of the children could be sent to live with other relatives or even be adopted by them. Many youngsters went into service at quite a young age so might be living with their employer's family.

Ann was born in 1824 in Wooldale. In 1851, she and her husband, John Whitworth, had a young servant named Hannah Kippas. They had ten children. By 1861 they had moved from Cartworth to Birds Edge Mill. Their eldest daughter, Emma, 12, was no longer living with them, which suggests she was working as a live-in servant elsewhere.

They moved from Birds Edge to Quarmby Fold and Ann stayed there until her death in 1914 at the age of 90. John died some time before 1881, but daughters Clara and Louise Ann and son Sam continued living with their mother. All the others had left. Emma married Abraham Townend in 1872, but continued living in the Quarmby Fold area. In 1879, her husband died leaving her a widow with four small children. She moved back to live with her mother. The cottage now housed four adults as Clara and Sam were still at home, plus Emma's four children, aged between 7 and 1. Shortly after this, Sam got married and moved out, but Ann's granddaughter, Louise Ann, moved in. All the women, except Ann, went into mills as menders, burlers or knotters. Ann probably provided the child-minding service that enabled the girls to work.

In Quarmby Fold, which consisted of approximately thirty-two households, six of them were occupied by widows. The other four were as follows:

Hannah Kitson, born in 1845, was a dressmaker, living on her own and working for herself, most likely from home.

Elizabeth was born in 1849 in Penistone. She married George Varey, who was twenty-one years older than herself. They lived with their three children Mary, Thomas and Hannah, but George died in 1880. Elizabeth moved to Lindley. Thomas had left home but Elizabeth, Mary and Hannah were all working as burlers in 1891. At the next census, Mary had left home and the household consisted of Elizabeth, her daughter Hannah, son-in-law John Lees and their child Elsie, who was only 3 months old. They had also taken in a boarder.

When Eliza Booth's husband died, she was left a widow with two young children. She was able to work as a worsted-mender but, to supplement their income, she took in two boarders, a worsted-weaver and a little girl of 9, Lilian Hoyle, who appears to be the daughter of Eliza's next-door neighbour. This was quite common and they may have been related.

Azubah Haggis moved from Halifax to Huddersfield where her husband was an overlooker and farmer. After he died, Azubah took over the farm. One son, Jabez, became a carter and carrier and another became a milk deliverer. The three daughters all went into local mills to earn their living.

Amalgamated families were common too. John Goostray, a boatman/bargee, married Mary Ann in 1875. They had two children, Sarah and Tom. Mary Ann died in 1882, in Huddersfield, leaving John with two small children to look after.

Mary Ellen Dyson married John Hinchliffe in 1871. They had five children: Annie, James, Harriet Ellen, Ethel and Albert. John died in 1884, leaving Mary Ellen with five small children and no means of support.

In 1886, John Goostray married Mary Ellen Hinchliffe, née Dyson, four years his senior. The two families lived together in St Andrews Road in 1891, by which time Annie and James Hinchcliffe were both working. By 1901, the family had moved to Lily Street. Annie and James had both left home, but all the other children were still there and working. Ten years later Tom had left home too, but the family had expanded to include James Walker, Harriet's husband, and their 2-year-old daughter Nellie. Ethel had married in 1907, but her husband died, so she was living with her mother and stepfather, under the name of Ramsden. Ethel and the three men were working, but not her mother or sister.

In this way, the permutations of the family were able to keep a reasonable standard of living, provide child-minding when needed and, hopefully, care for the parents into old age.

CHAPTER TWO

Quality of Life

The quality of life depended then as now on what you were able to earn, how much education you had and where you lived. The very poor could barely make ends meet, let alone have sufficient spare to employ another person to do their housework, so a servant in the household suggested the family income was higher. Many families, however, might have employed a daily help who would not show on the census.

One of Huddersfield's most notorious areas was around Castlegate. Looking at fifty-six houses on this street in 1851, the majority of inhabitants were working, some having businesses in which they employed others. Most came from Huddersfield district with a sprinkling of incomers from other counties of England and a few Irish.

Three were listed as lodging-houses, including that of Matilda Hardwick, though she only had two lodgers with her. Another had ten lodgers, but the largest had a hundred lodgers. Many households included one or two lodgers, in addition to a specified occupation, but did not refer to themselves as lodging-house-keepers. Seven houses had at least one servant, in addition to those working in the largest lodging-house. Only ten worked in jobs connected with the textile industry. As expected, in the centre of town there were service industry jobs – a baker, a clog-maker, grocers, tea-dealers, bread-baker, a bookseller, butcher, porter, shopkeepers and a pawnbroker. Others worked as joiners, plasterers and charwomen. There were three manufacturers: an umbrella maker, a stocking manufacturer and a tobacco pipe manufacturer.

Two women lived on the income from other houses. Betty Jowett was a 64-year-old widow, living with her daughter, Martha, and grandson, Joseph Aspinall. Neither adult gives any other occupation, but nearby is an area called Jowett's Court. This may be coincidence, or it may be that Betty owned some or all of the seven houses in that little court. All the houses there were occupied by semi-skilled workers.

Forty years later there were fewer families in the area. There had been large slum clearances and a clampdown on letting rooms to lodgers. The number of Irish had risen and there were more unskilled workers, such as general labourers and rag-sorters. Only two houses had servants, both run by women: Harriet McGrath, who was a 'landlady' with thirty-two lodgers and two servants, and Bridget Walsh, a public house-keeper who had just four lodgers and one servant. One woman was listed 'living on own means', which could mean anything from being a prostitute to having investments that paid good dividends.

Looking just a short distance away at St Paul's Street. Families here in 1851 were more likely to have servants and be skilled or white-collar workers, such as clerks, builders and drapers. There were three professionals – an architect, an accountant and a veterinary surgeon. Louise Roebuck, wife of plumber and glazier John, gave her occupation as milliner. She also employed two assistants: Henrietta Wilkinson from Beverley and Mary Briggs from Hertfordshire, who was a bonnet maker.

By 1901, the area had changed, with some skilled or white-collar workers, but no professionals. Nor did any household employ a servant. Some, particularly women, took in a few lodgers. Elizabeth Meller was an ironmonger's clerk, presumably working for her father, who was an ironmonger.

Two women worked for themselves and were employers. Priscilla Gledhill was a widow working as a window cleaner. There is no evidence as to whether she went out cleaning the windows herself or simply employed others to do so. Living with her in 1901 were her daughter Clara, a weaver, and John Rhodes, who was a working window cleaner.

Selina Stott was another widow who was left enough capital to open a marine store, supplying goods to bargees who worked on the canal through Aspley. She had three daughters: Aimie or Minnie, who was born in Chicago in 1872, a dressmaker; Agnes, born in Huddersfield in 1877, a teacher; and Annetta, who became a clerk in the marine store.

Poverty and the workhouse

Workhouses were built in each district or Poor Law Union. Outdoor Relief did continue, but those in need were supposed to go into the workhouse. There they were sent into different wards – male, female and children. This system lasted until the twentieth century.

In 1850, the government inspectors reported on the situation in Huddersfield, where small workhouses were found in Almondbury, Kirkheaton, Honley and Golcar as well as in Huddersfield town itself. The inspectors condemned each of these. Only Huddersfield had any kind of sick ward, none had proper provision for the different categories of paupers, nor was there any provision for pregnant women or babies.[32]

A new workhouse was eventually built at Deanhouse in 1862. The Hinchcliffes were appointed as master and mistress in 1877, with a salary of £100, to be split £60/£40.[33]

In 1871, the Local Government Board became responsible for the administration of the workhouse, though the day-to-day running remained under the control of the local board of guardians. The new inspectorate emphasised care rather than just controlling the poor, but it was not until 1872 that a new workhouse in Crosland Moor was built and the smaller workhouses closed. The workhouse at Birkby became an isolation hospital.

Closing the smaller workhouses caused the unemployment of most of the workers – outsiders were brought in to run the new establishments. In 1872, Mrs Kenworthy, matron at Kirkheaton, petitioned the board of governors for a pension. This was debated, but considered too expensive and she was awarded only a single payment of £5. She was 54 years old, so a new job, with board and lodgings, would have been difficult to find.[34]

In 1908, pensions were introduced for those over 70 years of age, which helped keep some old people out of the workhouse. Limited unemployment and illness benefits were brought in under the 1911 National Insurance Act, though this only applied to certain workers, which meant primarily men, and didn't cover all industries. Their families and non-workers were not covered.

After the First World War, unemployment rose as soldiers were demobbed. An 'Out of Work Donation' was paid as a temporary benefit at a rate of 29 shillings (£1.45) for men and 24 shillings (£1.20) for women, even if they were both in the same circumstances. This was ended by 1920 when the Unemployment Insurance Act extended the unemployment benefits to more workers and for a longer period of time. The Widows, Orphans and Old Age Contributory Pensions Act of 1925 reduced the pension age to 65 and widows finally gained a small pension based on their husbands' contributions.

Other benefits included the family allowance, introduced in 1945, and the National Insurance Act of 1946, which brought in or consolidated a range of benefits. It did not, however, provide those benefits to married women, even if working. The 1948 National Health Act ensured that all could obtain free medical treatment.

The Local Government Act of 1929 allowed for the abolition of the workhouse. Many were renamed public assistance institutions and continued to provide similar care, while others developed into hospitals or old people's homes.

Orphanages

Ragged schools were set-up to deal with very poor street urchins. In Huddersfield, one was set-up in Fitzwilliam Street in 1861.[35] The trustees, twelve men and twelve women, were drawn from the Protestant religion, though it was the women who actually ran the school on a day-to-day basis. Two of the longest serving trustees were Miss M.M. Hirst of Greenhead Cottage and Eliza Mellor. The children were taught the basics and also fed at the school. Later it changed to being an industrial home. The ladies of the committee visited the school once a week, taking it in turns to be the 'visitor' each month, and undertook to visit the homes of new scholars, absent scholars and needy cases who had applied to attend. They were also responsible for finding funds for the school, so divided up the town into sections, each lady being responsible for canvassing their area for support.

In 1879, Mary Ann Grant was appointed matron of the school at a salary of £50 per annum. Her husband Peter was to assist her in cleaning the windows, etc, at no expense to the charity, as he was not an employee. The children did not just get a basic education, they were trained in various industrial occupations and, in so doing, earned money for the school. All other finances had to come from fundraising and subscriptions. The girls learned domestic subjects. When they did leave school and start work, their wages went to pay for their board, though they were allowed 6d (2p) a week pocket money. In addition, family and friends were expected, where possible, to contribute towards their upkeep.

Mary Bickerstaff was appointed in 1885, after Mrs Grant left, at the same salary of £50 per annum. She was allowed a holiday each year, usually of ten days, and given a 'gift' of 3 guineas (£3.15) to help with transport. She was also allowed extra help in the form of a washerwoman one day a week and a charwoman for three days. After five years work, the committee was so pleased with her efforts that they allowed her to eat with the children instead of having to provide her own food.

By 1900, the buildings needed substantial refurbishment. Renamed the Huddersfield Orphan Home, it had accommodation for fifty children with lesson rooms, dining room, girls' and boys' dormitories with twenty-five beds in each, though at the time there were more girls than boys in the home. There were two staircases provided in case of fire.

Miss Mary Bickerstaff, matron, remained at the orphanage until it closed in 1924, retiring at the age of 76. The minute books available do not record her ever having had a pay rise, but remaining on the amount paid originally to Mrs Grant in 1879.

Matilda Pyrah

Matilda Faux worked as a children's nurse until she married John Pyrah. She was voted onto the board of guardians in 1894, under the new Local Government Act, and took an active part in her duties, particularly in her dealings with the workhouse, being on both the visiting and selection committees for Crosland Moor Workhouse. When expenditure on a new maternity wing came up, she was one of the many who voted for the idea, even though others felt there was already far too much being spent there. In addition, she visited Wadsley Asylum near Sheffield to check on the treatment of the mentally ill who had been sent there from Huddersfield.

Matilda opposed the provision of a wagonette for those guardians who lived some distance from the railway stations, saying they, including the women, should pay for themselves or walk. When it was suggested that a special chair should be bought for the chairman, costing £13 or £14, almost a year's wages for a working man, she objected strongly, suggesting that it should be paid for by subscription and those who voted for it should be the first to put their names down. Needless to say, the idea was dropped.

She pushed for better education for children and better training opportunities. Later she was involved in establishing the cottage homes for children, served on the old age pension committee and was one of the first members of the Victoria Nurses Association.

She was a very keen Liberal, being one of a group of ladies who met in 'Joseph Woodhead's library' and helped formed Huddersfield Women's Liberal Association. She continued her active public life to the end and became the oldest member of the Yorkshire Liberal Association. She died in 1941.[36]

The Board of Health

During the nineteenth century, there were epidemics of cholera and typhus. The Public Health Act 1848 established local boards of health to deal with street cleaning, sewerage and water supplies.

Mrs Hannah Micklethwaite, of Johnny Moore Hill, Paddock, was seriously ill in a cholera epidemic in 1848 but survived. Her son, Allen, aged 17, died on 21 September; her husband, John, aged 44, died on 22 September, and Richard Berry, engaged to look after the family, died on 30 September. According to other reports another nurse of hers died and a second son, probably John, who would have been 18 at the time of the cholera outbreak.[37]

The 1851 census shows that Hannah Micklethwaite was still living in the area with her three remaining sons. Many other women on Johnny Moore Hill were widows with no occupation but shown as head of household, often with children living with them and, presumably, providing financial support.

Over the years the local boards were given more and more powers: providing public bathing houses, naming streets, preventing fires and removing dangerous buildings or obstructions in the street.

In 1913, a health publicity week was held with Mrs Mary Blamires presiding over the opening event. She said 'it was a privilege to be a representative of the women of the town'. Others on the platform that day included women who also appeared on the committees of the majority of Huddersfield's charitable works: Lady Raynor, Miss Emily Siddon, Mrs C.F. Sykes, Mrs Demetriadi, Mrs Studdard, Miss Broadbent, Mrs Donkersley, Mrs J.M. Roberts, Mrs Edgar Dyson, Mrs Rhodes, Mrs Matilda Pyrah, Mrs John Fisher, Miss Irving, Mrs Bannister, Mrs T. Shires, Mrs Alfred Roberts, Mrs Roberts and Mrs Baines. After listening to the discussion of how to improve health, Miss Siddon pointed out that housing reform and providing 'proper living accommodation' were the keys to seeing the improvements in health hoped for in the town.[38]

Medical practitioners

Male doctors put every barrier they could before women to prevent them qualifying as doctors. Some women qualified abroad, so the medical profession refused to accept medical degrees not taken in Britain. Under the 1876 Medical (Qualifications) Act, a medical degree had to be granted to all qualified applicants regardless of sex.

The Association of Medical Women began three years later with only nine members, the total number of women qualified as doctors in Britain. This association eventually developed into the Medical Women's Federation. By 1901, the census showed over 200 female doctors in the UK.

In 1905, Huddersfield was one of the few areas to have health visitors. All new mothers were visited at home by qualified women to give advice to try to reduce infant deaths. Dr Prudence Elizabeth Gaffikin was assistant medical officer of health, along with Dr Catherine Laura Boyd. A team of eighty volunteer health visitors also visited new mothers. One shilling (5p) was given for each birth reported to the medical officer of health within twenty-four hours of the birth. The Huddersfield Corporation Act, passed in 1906, allowed them to insist on notification of birth. By 1915, this Act had been made compulsory and applied nationally. During both world wars, restrictions on women practising medicine were lifted and more women were able to qualify, though it was 1947 before all medical colleges became co-educational.

The Crimean War (1853-56) changed the country's attitude to nursing. In 1919, the Nursing Registration Act required all nurses to be registered, and training became more formal. Under the 1948 National Health Act, most hospitals and mental institutions became nationally controlled, though district nurses were the responsibility of the county council.

Charities helped provide nursing for the poor in their own home. In 1887, the Women's Jubilee Fund provided training and support for nurses to work with those who were unable to pay for treatment themselves. In 1897, this became the

Queen Victoria's Jubilee Nurses and, in 1928, the Queen's Institute of District Nursing. Huddersfield Queen Victoria Nurses Association became affiliated to the national group in 1897.

Jessie Murray

Jessie was born in Plymouth in 1855 to an upper-middle-class family, which included her sister Florence, later to come to Huddersfield, marry Josiah Lockwood and become known for the diary she left of her time here. In 1890, Jessie came to Huddersfield to set-up a nursing home, which was set-up on Trinity Street and was successful, regularly advertising in *The Nursing Record* for experienced nurses.

Jessie Murray died in November 1905, aged 50. She was described as having a 'striking personality' and being very devout. The church was filled with more than twenty-five of her nurses, as well as many of the local well-to-do who had come to appreciate her work as 'head ... of an establishment which carried with it so much anxiety and responsibility'.[39]

Elsie May Harling, née Hallas[40]

Elsie was born in 1899 in Crosland Moor. She trained as a nurse in Halifax, with a three-month probationary period during which she received no pay, just board and lodgings. At the end of this, she signed a three-year contract, which had an exit fee of £10 – over half her annual salary of £18.

Her duties began at 7 am with cleaning the wards, polishing the brass bedsteads and wiping each leaf on the aspidistra. Sweet cocoa was made for each patient and, when necessary, patients were escorted down to theatre. Elsie had to stay throughout the operation and escort them back again, 'the nurse must never leave her patient'.

Nurses worked a seventy-two-hour week with two hours off-duty per day, during which time they had to attend lectures. Sunday was a half-day holiday, plus one day per month and three weeks holiday per year.

Dorothy Wood[41]

Dorothy was born in 1902 and became a Queen's Nurse, which equipped her to become a health visitor and school nurse.

In 1932, the local branch of the College of Nursing offered a scholarship of £100 for a State Registered nurse to go to Canada for six months to study any branch of nursing work. Dorothy won the scholarship and set off for Canada. In Toronto and Montreal she stayed with local nurses, studying their system of health visiting. On her return she gave talks to nurses in Huddersfield and wrote letters to the *Nursing Times* about her experiences in Canada.

The first local clinic opened in 1927 in Marsden, giving free health advice to mothers, with a doctor and nurse attending each Thursday afternoon. The average attendance was eighty mothers and babies.

Dorothy retired in 1956. In 1996, she became the victim of an apparent burglary that went wrong and she died of injuries received. No one has ever been convicted of the murder of a woman who spent her life caring for thousands of children.

Medical care in Huddersfield

Until the National Health Service began after the Second World War, all medical assistance had to be paid for: doctors, nurses, medicines, maternity. As the nineteenth century progressed, more responsibility was taken over by the local authorities, or by charities.

Huddersfield Royal Infirmary

Huddersfield Royal Infirmary (HRI) started as a charitable dispensary set-up in 1814. The Huddersfield and Upper Agbrigg Hospital opened in 1831 as a public charity, to help the poor sick unable to pay for treatment themselves, though a contribution was expected. When the hospital needed funds, the committee knew exactly who to go to: 'they would appeal to the ladies, whose benevolence had been so signally proved by the late bazaar.' The bazaar had been organised and run by women, others supported by sending goods and funds for the event. From then on it was the ladies who organised the fundraising.[42] The hospital remained on New North Road until the 1960s, when it removed to Lindley.

Miss Emily Barry was matron between 1901 and 1923. In 1918, national scholarships were established for training sister tutors. One of the first to be awarded was to Miss M.A. Abram, assistant matron at HRI.

Mill Hill Hospital/Huddersfield Isolation Hospital

There was a sanatorium wing at HRI in 1881 and an isolation hospital at Birkby from the old workhouse, but these were intended to be temporary solutions. In 1887, there was an outbreak of scarlet fever, a potentially fatal disease. The Birkby site could house only fifty-four, so patients were put two or three in a bed. At a local council meeting, the mayor pointed out that 'most of them had a house in which they could isolate any member of their family who was attacked by disease … there were thousands of houses in Huddersfield incapable of any such provision and it was from them that the great dangers of infection arose'.[43] Mill Hill Hospital was the answer to the problem.

Bradley Wood Sanatorium was also built as an isolation hospital, later specialising in the treatment of tuberculosis. It closed in 1978.

The hospitals worked together to ensure that nurses in the area received a range of experiences during their training:

> *On the recommendation of the Education and Examination Committee the application from the authorities of St Luke's Hospital, Huddersfield, that the combined Scheme of Training extending over a period of four years, under which the probationers of St Luke's Hospital will spend a portion of their training in St Luke's Hospital, Royal Infirmary, Mill Hill Isolation Hospital and Bradley Wood Sanatorium, be approved.*[44]

Princess Royal Maternity Hospital

This was originally an old vicarage, extended and improved by the council and opened in 1928 as the Municipal Maternity Home, providing twenty beds. In 1939, a new extension was opened by the Princess Royal, Princess Mary, and the name of the hospital was changed in her honour. It became a midwifery school but closed in 1974.

Workhouse hospitals

As well as providing shelter for the poor and homeless, workhouses provided basic hospital care. Crosland Moor Workhouse had a hospital with seventy-two beds and an infections ward for twenty.

In 1897, the Nurses in Workhouses Order stated that no pauper nurse (i.e. unqualified) was to be employed in the workhouse except as an assistant. At least one qualified superintendent nurse per three assistant nurses had to be employed, with at least three years' experience in nursing.

In 1913, the workhouses were renamed as poor law institutions. When the workhouse was transferred to Huddersfield Corporation in 1930, the name was changed to St Luke's Hospital, providing mainly geriatric care.

Treatment of the disabled

The blind

As well as congenital blindness or accident, blindness could be caused by smallpox or scarlet fever – diseases that were prevalent in the nineteenth century. The Society for the Instruction of the Blind was formed in 1856 in Huddersfield to give elementary instruction to nearly forty blind people in their own homes. It was particularly important for girls to be trained in some way since blind women rarely married. It was assumed that they would not be able to cope with running a home or raising children.

By 1883, the society rented rooms in town, with a large library of volumes in raised type for the blind to borrow or read. A class was held there every Wednesday to teach children how to read them. Also studied were writing in Braille, geography with raised maps, and arithmetic. Two children went to Royal Normal College at Upper Norwood and one to the York School for the Blind. Fifty-three people received instruction: seventeen were readers, eighteen received books and eighteen were visited at home. There was a choir of blind children with their instructress, Miss Devine. At one meeting, Rev Bardsley suggested everyone should contribute towards the education of a girl called Annie Parker. She was blind, but her parents were unable to pay for her to attend any specialist school.[45]

The following year Mrs Bardsley became president. It was reported that Annie Parker had been accepted at Sheffield College for the Blind, paid for with the money raised at the previous annual meeting. The treasurer, Mrs Tomlinson, detailed the state of the society's funds.[46]

The statement was probably timely. In 1886, an appeal was made for more funds. Miss Devine was still teaching at Lord Street, mainly children and a number of adults. Alice Healey was being funded to stay at the Royal Normal College, Norwood, and Annie Parker at Sheffield College. Another girl was ready for Norwood, but the committee didn't have sufficient funds to send her, though they were hoping to get the parents to pay some and make up the rest by getting more subscribers to raise the necessary money. It was suggested that fifty young ladies in the society should each raise one pound in order to send Eliza Williamson to college and secure for her a thorough musical education. The funds were eventually forthcoming for her to go to London.

The teacher's report explained that all, except Eliza Williamson, were beginners. She wanted to encourage the attendance of blind children in ordinary elementary schools, as mixing with other children would stimulate them more. Rev J.W. Town said there was a blind girl in the church school at Lindley and she was a very bright and intelligent child. A great deal might be taught to blind children by listening to the other children.[47]

In 1893, a new law compelled parents to send disabled children to school. This affected local school boards as they had to make provision for such children. The Act applied to deaf children aged 7 to 16 and to blind children aged 5 to 16.

In 1948, a home for homeless blind people was opened at The Holly, New Hey Road. With space for twelve people, there were already ten residents when it opened. It was hoped to increase the rooms for up to twenty people once wartime restrictions on building were lifted.[48]

The deaf

In the nineteenth century, the general term for the hearing impaired was 'deaf and dumb'. There was no distinction made between those who were hard of hearing, those who had lost hearing later in life and those who were deaf from birth and therefore unable to speak, since there was little proper training for them. Another term often used was 'mutes' or 'deaf mutes'. These terms also appeared on census returns.

In Huddersfield, the Deaf and Dumb Association (HDDA), established in 1872, provided support and a clubroom for meetings. The ladies on the committee were: Mrs Huth, Mrs Scott (Melbourne House) Mrs G.W. Tomlinson, Mrs Whitman, Mrs W.J. Kaye, Miss Lowenthal and Miss Mallinson. In later years, Miss Siddon joined the committee. Mrs Huth, who had learned sign language, was chosen as the principal delegate to go to London and report to a royal commission into provision for the disabled.

The association helped find work for the deaf, mainly in mills but also apprenticing them to trades. It tried to integrate the deaf into ordinary society. Some religious services were held in the rooms in Albion Street, 'conducted in their own language' because the deaf felt they couldn't participate in church services.[49]

Mental disability

In 1845, the government made it compulsory for local authorities to set-up county asylums for the poor with a mental disability. There was no distinction between mental illnesses such as schizophrenia and mental disability such as Downs Syndrome. It was difficult to obtain suitably qualified nurses for the asylums, particularly for women. Better educated women tended to avoid training as nurses for the mentally ill, possibly because they felt they would come into closer contact with the working classes.

Women were seen as having less mental stability than men. This lesser capacity could be disturbed by an excess of studying, too much exercise, or by eating highly stimulating food. Certifying to 'madness', as it was called then, required only the signature of two doctors. Since all doctors were men, it was relatively easy for them to dismiss as 'mad' any women showing signs of behaviour outside the male view of what was correct for females, including wanting to take advantage of the 1857 Divorce Act. Other signs of madness encompassed post-natal depression or the menopause, epilepsy, moral insanity (i.e. adultery or any sexual behaviour outside marriage), or even disobedience of the father's dicta. Any outburst of crying or anger was seen as 'madness' in a woman. If kept at home, she was confined to her room and given bland food, little stimulation, such as reading, and ordered to rest. Once in an institution, treatments could include cold baths, sedatives or mercury and antimony. The latter kept the women feeling ill, so they were less likely to be violent. Single women were a threat because they were not always specifically under the control of men and even lesbianism was seen as a form of madness.

It was also believed that any kind of mental illness manifested itself in physical symptoms. Those who had difficulty in moving, speaking or had epilepsy were considered to be mentally ill too.

Jane Walker[50]

Jane was admitted to the West Riding Pauper Lunatic Asylum in Wakefield just after her second son was born.

This was the first time she had been in the asylum and it was noted that she was not epileptic or suicidal. She could read and write, but was listed as being 'insane for eight weeks'. The supposed cause was weakness. Treatment consisted of purgatives and sedatives that had a 'decided benefit to her bodily health'. At the end of November, she was discharged as 'recovered'.

In November 1866 she was admitted again, this time suffering from 'moroseness, depression of spirits, refusal of all food'. She 'attempted violence upon her husband and others, imagines all is on fire about her, there is incoherency in her speech, talks wildly about her children'.

She was discharged in May 1867, but re-admitted in February 1869. She was: 'too much annoyed at having been deceived when she was brought here as they told her they were taking her somewhere else. She has been silent for nearly six months hardly ever speaking. Her husband is a drunkard and he has been made melancholy by his poverty and insufficiency of food. She is prone to cry. She has a melancholy look.'

The cause of her mental illness was put down to the fact that she was going through the menopause. She was discharged in October 1869, after a stay of eight months. It is likely that Jane spent the rest of her life in and out of the Asylum.

Storthes Hall

In 1904, the Storthes Hall estate was bought by the West Riding County Council as the fourth asylum for the area, specifically for pauper lunatics. Annual wages for the female staff when the hall first opened were set at £20 for charge nurses, plus board, lodgings, uniform and washing. Female attendants were paid £18, plus £3 extra for night duty, working an average of eighty-seven hours a week.

The marriage bar applied to female workers, leading to a constant change of staff, many of whom were inexperienced in mental health nursing. Training for mental health nurses was non-existent until the mid-nineteenth century, when it became a separate branch of nursing, including the study of pathology and management of patients in the training. Staff were initially called attendants, but after full training became called chargehands.

Storthes Hall became known as Storthes Hall Mental Hospital between 1929 and 1938, changing then to the West Riding Mental Hospital between 1939 and 1948, and the Storthes Hall Hospital from 1949 to its closure in 1991.[51]

The physically disabled

Disability could be caused by diseases such as poliomyelitis, rickets or cerebral palsy, or by accidents in the home or at work. Compensation was rarely forthcoming for industrial accidents until almost the end of the nineteenth century. Any help given was either charitable or through poor relief. While there were organisations to help the deaf or blind, few concentrated on the physically disabled and there were few special schools or training establishments for them.

The Disability Employment Act of 1944 did provide for sheltered employment. Remploy had its beginnings in 1945, when it was known as the Disabled Person's Employment Corporation, offering sheltered employment to severely disabled people. Later it developed into a modern-day recruitment and employment services agency for disabled people and those with barriers to employment. A Remploy factory was established in Huddersfield in January 1948 on Brook Street.

Pensions

Though some people received pensions from early times, the pension depended very much on the job that was done and the goodwill of the employer. Other groups set-up their own benefit funds, such as the Huddersfield Trades Benevolent Fund in 1890, to provide pensions for their members. When Joshua Blackburn died, his widow Martha was granted the pension. The committee considered ten candidates for two further pensions, finally allocating them to Joseph Lister, and Frances Sophia Walker, widow of Thomas Walker.[52]

A National Pension Fund for Nurses began in 1887. Nurses paid into the fund and could draw a pension at the age of 65. The nurses' pension was not a charity, nor was it confined just to nurses, but was for all 'sickness workers'. Men, however, were not eligible for the donations bonus fund, as that was reserved for women.[53]

Teachers' pensions were introduced in the 1890s, and a scheme applying to all civil servants in the 1920s. National pensions were introduced by Lloyd George in 1909, for those over 70 years of age. They were open to both men and women who had worked all their lives and were 'of good character'. Most of the first recipients were women because they tend to live longer. The pension was only 5 shillings (25p) per week, but it was set at such a high age very few actually lived long enough to draw it. The low level of benefits was supposed to encourage people to save for their old age, despite the fact that much of the working-class were unable to save anything. Women received a lower pension on the grounds that they had fewer responsibilities, despite the fact that they often had to support parents or siblings as well.

A contributory pension scheme was introduced in 1925, and this included cover for some widows and orphans. From 1929, widows were able to draw the pension at age 55.

By 1940, benefits were given to unmarried women who had paid into the scheme and the wives of insured male pensioners. Women's pension age was reduced to 60, but women's contributions were increased. In 1946, the contributory state pension became a flat rate for all.

However, widows drew their pension at age 55, but unmarried women didn't receive theirs until age 60. The National Spinsters Pension Association (NSPA), formed in Bradford in 1935, lobbied for spinsters to receive their pension at 55 too. The Huddersfield branch of the NSPA was formed soon after.

In their view, women were often forced to retire earlier than men because of their health or because some employers would not employ older women. Unmarried women often gave up work to look after parents. When their parents died, they were unable to find employment again. In 1936, the government decided against the demands of the NSPA. The MPs (all men) told them that if pensions were paid to spinsters at age 55 in the same way as widows were, then all women would want the same, which would be far too expensive.[54]

A government enquiry found that unemployment by unmarried women over 45 was higher than that of men. The enquiry drew attention to the number of women who ended up in dire poverty as a result of having to care for relatives. Ivy Littlewood, a sister at the Royal Infirmary, said that during her ten years nursing, forty per cent of the women she'd treated for cancer had been spinsters aged over 45. She could nurse the illness, but not treat the financial difficulties. The women could all have had treatment earlier but were afraid of losing their job or they simply could not afford to pay for treatment in the first place.[55]

The NSPA continued its fight, organising a rally in London, which many women from Huddersfield attended, setting off from St George's Square to join the London train. They arrived in Kings Cross for the rally in Kingsway Hall and Hyde Park. Despite their efforts, the government refused to change their stance, leaving many older women in poverty.

CHAPTER THREE

Working Life

For some women, work was a necessity, for others it brought the family just above the subsistence level of the man's wage. Objections to women working were not just from men. Single women complained that married women should stay at home, leaving jobs for those who needed them. Some married women felt there was a certain status in being able to remain at home looking after the house instead of having to go out to work. This did not, of course, take into account the married women who had been deserted or whose husband was ill and unable to work. Only the well-off could afford to stay in education long enough to gain qualifications needed for the higher paid, higher status jobs. This left many genteel single women all competing for similar posts.

Domestic service

Domestic service was one of the largest areas of employment for women. Some children lived with their employers and acted as a general servant, doing all the hard work of the household. Walter Vickerman, a woollen cloth manufacturer at Almondbury, kept two servants: one house servant, Sarah Haigh, and a nurse for his little girl, though the nurse, Caroline Kaye, was only 13 years old herself.

The workhouse found domestic service a useful outlet for their younger inmates. In 1873, the board of guardians had a complaint from Mrs Beaumont regarding Hannah Hodgson, a girl who had been sent to work for her. Mrs Beaumont had sent the girl to work in a local mill, confiscated her wages and still insisted she do all the housework in the evenings as well. The guardians were indignant and agreed that in future it should be made very clear that girls sent out as domestic servants should be kept solely as domestic servants.[56]

In 1880, the idea of industrial training for girls was mooted. An industrial trainer would be employed so that 'they should be taught how to sew, knit, wash, scour, bake etc'. This would prevent many of the girls being returned from their work placements and 'so that at eleven years of age they would be fit to go out to service, instead of being kept till twelve or thirteen years of age doing nothing towards their own maintenance'.[57]

Governesses were often well-to-do ladies who were unable to find a husband. Since women were excluded from most occupations, becoming a governess was one of their few options. However, they were not 'servants' like the maids or cook, nor were they on a social level with their employer.

After each world war, domestic servants were in short supply. Women had been working for higher wages and shorter hours. More, and better, job opportunities opened up. In Huddersfield, a training centre for domestic employment opened in Park Drive in 1931. The women were paid 12 shillings (60p) a week if between the ages of 18 and 20, with £1 per week if over 21. Lessons included cookery, laundry, housework and needlework, though the women had to pay 2 to 3 shillings (10-15p) per week for the cost of the garments they were making for themselves.[58]

After the First World War, women were directed into domestic service, particularly if claiming the dole (unemployment benefit). Women who had had other jobs paid National Insurance and became eligible for a pension and unemployment benefit. If they took up domestic service, they lost both these benefits, yet if they refused to do the work, they lost the benefit anyway.

The government published a dole report that wanted to reduce both contributions and benefits, but was especially hard on married women who, it said, were claiming benefit but not actually intending to return to work. Married women, therefore, had to convince the clerks that they did want to work. Women paid 1d (1/2p) less per week contribution than men did, but received 2 shillings (10p) less in benefits.

Private schools

Hypathia Wilson and her younger sister Jessica set-up a school, advertising it in Kelly's 1858 Trade Directory. Both sisters came from Huddersfield, as did one of their boarders on the 1861 census, while other boarders came from Middlesex and Scotland. There were thirteen women in the same directory, all running small schools, and four of them took in boarders too.

In Kelly's Directory for 1854, women are found running private schools, as confectioners, managing inns and acting as tea-dealers. Thirty-two traded as milliners and a further thirteen were straw-hat makers. Twenty-seven were shopkeepers. No women were listed as solicitors or accountants as these jobs were barred to them until just before the Second World War.

Ann Beaumont and Sarah Bottomley were both butchers. Lydia Moseley was an upholsterer and Ann Dunn and Mrs Rothwell were both Heald, Reed and Sley makers (these were parts of a loom). It is probable that those owning manufactories had inherited the business from their spouse and would have a male manager to run the day-to-day affairs, but it is difficult to find out the truth about how much hands-on work the women did.

Looking at the directories for 1900, women appear mainly in similar industries, such as dressmaking, millinery, innkeeping and general shopkeepers. Mrs Ann Marshall was a print-seller and fine art dealer on New Street and Mrs Elizabeth Kirby was a cigar merchant. Eight women ran dining and coffee rooms, and of the twenty people advertising apartments for rent, all were women.

As mechanisation increased, more jobs in factories became possible to women. The work became lighter and as women were paid less than men, they were more profitable. Engineering particularly was able to take on more women. Electrically driven machines meant the work could be broken down into sections, each part being done by unskilled or semi-skilled workers, many of them women. Growth in electrical production and telecommunications also provided jobs for women.

Local businesses

These ranged in size from sole traders to large companies which, over the years, became household names. Most businesses required some capital to set-up, which was beyond the means of the majority of women.

Innkeepers and beersellers

A trade which many women seem to have been involved in, and was, in many cases, considered quite 'respectable' was that of innkeeper. In Kelly's 1854 Trade Directory, there were ten women running pubs in the town centre. Many of the women who are listed as innkeepers had taken over the inn from their husbands, but this was not always the case.

The Great Western Inn at Marsden was an exceptionally busy inn as many people would drive out there on bank holidays. Nathaniel Bottomley came from Saddleworth to run the Great Western Inn. His wife Nanny (or Nancy) came with him and when Nathaniel died, she took over the inn and is listed as innkeeper in White's 1847 Trade Directory.

However, when she married William Rhodes, he took over the licence and became the innkeeper. When William died, the licence went back to his widow, this time in the name of Nanny Rhodes. Her granddaughter, Georgiana Wood, lived with her as domestic help. When Nanny Rhodes died, the whole of the Wood family moved into the Great Western Inn. Daniel Wood was the head of household and a farmer, but Georgiana was given as the innkeeper in the 1871 census. On Daniel's death, Georgiana became the head of household, rather than Daniel's widow as would be usual. Georgiana left the inn at the beginning of the twentieth century, but remained in Marsden until her death.

Mary Hellowell Carter

John Hellowell Carter, iron founder and engineer, became bankrupt in 1840 but managed to start up in trade again, appearing in Kelly's 1854 Trade Directory. By 1856 his wife Mary was left a widow. She was aged 40 and had given birth to at least ten children. She then set-up in business herself as a dealer in India rubber and gutta percha (another kind of rubber). She continued in this trade for many years, later taking in two of her sons, until she retired in 1891 to live 'on her own means'.

Thomas Broadbent, Engineering

This business was started in 1864, later moving to the Central Ironworks on Chapel Hill. In 1859, Thomas married Ellen Crabtree (often given as Helen) and they had seven children. Unfortunately, in 1880, Thomas died unexpectedly of typhoid fever. Rather than selling the business and investing the proceeds, Ellen decided to keep it to pass on to her sons. Somehow, she raised the capital needed and successfully ran the business for at least a further five years. In the 1881 census, her occupation is given as machine maker. The business is now internationally known for the quality of its products and still has its head office in Huddersfield.

Hanson Logistics

Joseph Hanson had a farm in Longwood. His wife Mary commandeered some of his horses and sons Joseph and Thomas, who were drafted into the budding carrier business. After her husband's death Mary continued to run the farm and developed the carrier work. She is listed in the 1838 and 1847 White's Trade Directories as being a 'carrier to Huddersfield, daily' from Longwood. Mary's descendants went on to develop this into an international business, but it started in Huddersfield, thanks to the resourcefulness of one woman.

Textiles

The textile industry spread as mills were built in almost every district around Huddersfield. The 1847 Factory Act, restricting the working hours of women and girls to ten hours per day, shows how prevalent female labour was and how hard they worked.

By 1861, more than 2,000 women were employed in some form in the mills. This rose to around 12,000 by 1891, and more than 22,000 in 1911. The textile industry was one of the biggest employers of women in Huddersfield. Their main jobs were in spinning, preparation and finishing, such as mending. Most mills were set-up by men as they were the ones who owned the capital, but one of the biggest firms owed its continued existence to a woman. When John Sykes died, his widow Charlotte took over and it was she who built the massive Acre Mill in Lindley (now part of the hospital).

Over the years, many jobs became mechanised and women were able to take over some jobs done previously by men. Though the power changed, the essentials of the job remained the same. But the controllers – overlookers, foremen, managers – were always men until well into the twentieth century.

Very little changed over the years with regard to the hierarchy of work. Men were still in the higher paid, supervisory or management capacity, women did the less skilled, less well-paid work. It was not until 1945 that the Huddersfield Juvenile Advisory Committee had 'for the first time been able to persuade the textile industry to employ girl labour in cloth designing'. They were quick to point out, though, that this was 'not an attempt to displace any man [but] to bring a fresh mind to bear'. There was also an early comment on equal pay: 'Women doing the same job as men are entitled to the same remuneration.'[59]

Shop work

Shops opened around seven in the morning, to allow time for getting everything ready, staying open until seven or eight at night for six days a week. The shop assistant had to stand all day, serving the customers, and would be expected to work until the last customer left, regardless of the time. At Christmas, holiday time or if a large order was received, they would also be expected to stay on until it was completed.

The Co-operative movement has a long history in Huddersfield, starting with its formation in 1829 in Westgate. In March 1860, the Huddersfield Industrial Co-operative Flour and Provision Society was established, setting up a grocery store in Buxton Road, with branches at Lindley and Moldgreen soon after.

The Co-operative Women's Guild was formed in 1892. Mrs Alfred Shaw was president, Mrs Merrifield treasurer, and Mrs Henry Hirst secretary. A later vice-president was Mrs Mary K. Marshall, who went on to become president in 1898, and she became chairman of the education committee, upon which she was the only woman. In July 1899, she went to the annual conference in Plymouth, where she read a lecture, *Women on Educational Committees*.

The Co-op was involved in philanthropic work, including education for children and adults. When examinations in 'Co-operation' were held in 1899, all eleven adult students passed. The three who passed at the highest level included Amy Balmforth. Amy worked in the drapery department, but despite her obvious commitment and ability, she had to leave six years later when she got married. The same happened to Miss Sykes, who was the manageress of the restaurant that opened in 1906 in Buxton Road.[60]

Rushworth's Department Store was established in the 1870s. During the First World War, they expanded their range of goods to include china, leather goods and other household items. Female staff were expected to wear long dark dresses, which they had to provide themselves. They were well trained in customer service, including how to deal with complaints. It was considered quite a prestigious job, often taking in girls from elite schools such as Greenhead High School. Just before the Second World War, the starting wage was 16 shillings (77p) per week. Hours worked were from 9 am to 6 pm, and to 8 pm on Saturdays, with a half-day off on Wednesday. Girls were sent to college for bookkeeping and poster display work. They were expected to know their regular customers and greet them by name.

When clothes rationing was brought in in 1940, the store adapted what it was selling to the times. On sale were dungarees, ladies trousers for ARP (Air Raid Precautions) duties, small torches, anti-splinter nets for sticking to windows to prevent glass flying everywhere during an air-raid, and blackout material. With the make do and mend attitude prevalent, Rushworth's offered a mending service too.

The majority of the female staff were unmarried, as was usual, until the 1950s, and few seem to have been appointed as managers to any of the departments during the early years.[61]

Early closing

The 1892 Shop Hours Act limited the total number of hours under-18s could work to seventy-four, including mealtimes. If they had another job, such as in a factory, the hours had to be added together and not exceed the statutory limit. In 1899, the Seats for Shop Assistants Act laid down that seats should be provided for female assistants. These Acts did not apply to members of a family employed in a shop.

The Shops Act of 1904 allowed local authorities to enforce early closing or a half-day a week. Since the shopkeepers themselves had to agree to this by a sixty-six percent majority, it was not very successful.

Sunday trading gradually ceased, but it was not until the Shop Hours Act of 1911 that shops were forced to close for a half-day during the week. This also reduced the number of hours worked to sixty.

Office work

By the late 1880s, many offices had at least one typewriter and it was found that women took to the work more easily than men. The main problem was how to accommodate women in the workplace. Separate offices and toilets had to be provided.

Initially, the work attracted well-educated middle-class women, who were expected to have high standards of English. As more women learned typewriting and office skills, the job became downgraded. Shorthand had originally been taught only to boys, but the technical colleges offered secretarial skills, including shorthand, to girls too.

One of the biggest employers of women was the Civil Service. When the Post Office took over the telegraph service, the existing female staff there became civil servants. The Postmaster General soon realised that he could employ better educated women for less money than men, that they were more amenable to work, and they wouldn't need to be paid as much pension as their length of service would be curtailed when they married. Not surprisingly, the number of female clerks increased. By the end of the century women workers could be found in many departments, including the Registrar General's Office, the Inland Revenue and the Board of Trade.

The First World War opened up opportunities for women to move into jobs normally done by men. By 1913, a lady clerk was employed in a bank, which was following the 'lead in Norway where they and lady typists are common'. The banker went on to say, 'we are all feminists in these days, militancy notwithstanding, but we must confess that the invasion of our precincts by the sex fills us with misgiving.'[62]

Jobs in building societies, banks and solicitors were considered the better type of office job, requiring girls who had a good education, spoke and dressed well: ideal for middle-class girls. Mr Edgar Sheard remembered a number of girls working in the offices of Armitage, Sykes and Hinchcliffe during and after the First World War:

> *There were three young ladies in the office: Miss B.M. Hinchliffe, who did Mr Sykes' work, Miss Mabel Battye, who did Mr Hinchcliffe's work and Miss Doris Nichol who was the telephonist.*
>
> *After the War the three ladies in the office left. Miss Edith Bates took over as Mr A.E.T. Hinchcliffe's secretary*

> *originally, but he decided to have a male secretary. Miss Bates became my secretary, a position which she filled with great loyalty and efficiency for forty years until her death. She did an enormous amount of work without complaint and was an ideal secretary. Others included Miss Marion Taylor who later went to another solicitor; Miss Molly Lee who was a rather "avant garde" type of young lady but very nice and I had many discussions with her on politics, religion, the arts and the like; Miss Dorothy Pearson, Miss Mildred Fielding, Miss Elsie Moore, who later went to the tax office and Miss Marjorie Shaw.*[63]

During the First World War, women clerks were taken on specifically to release men for the war. Afterwards, although many women did leave, others were kept on because they were already trained. A similar situation pertained during and after the Second World War, but with the advent of social reform, many more administration positions were created, frequently filled by women.

Telephonists

By 1912, a nationwide telephone service was offered by the Post Office. The switchboard was manual, with an operator connecting the lines. Women were favoured for the job, but not allowed to work night-shifts after 10 pm. They could attain the position of supervisor, in charge of half-a-dozen female operators. All had to be well-educated and above a set height in order to reach the highest row of sockets.

The Post Office started the first women-only association in the Civil Service in 1901: the Association of Post Office Women Clerks. In 1931, it amalgamated with the National Association of Women Civil Servants. In 1919, women telegraphists and telephonists could join the Union of Postal Workers. However much these unions tried to help women, they were up against the male dominated larger unions. In 1927, a speaker at the Post Office Controlling Officer Association commented: 'The telephone is rapidly taking over the telegraph service but women, who do the whole of the supervisory and manipulative work, are still barred from the highest positions.'[64]

Miss Ethel Shinton was appointed telephonist in 1909 at Huddersfield. She wore a headset to listen to callers, and 'juggled with the mass of communications under her control'. In 1912, the Post Office took over and effectively nationalised the telephone service. When Ethel retired in 1949, she said that the busiest times had been on Armistice Day in 1918 and at the end of the Second World War.[65]

Trade unions

There were a number of reasons why women didn't join unions. In many unions, the men wouldn't accept women members. Women were paid less and therefore the men felt this would bring down their own wages. They also conspired to keep women out of the skilled, highly paid jobs, especially in textiles where large numbers of women were employed. The lower pay meant that women rarely had the spare money for union subscriptions. Many women only worked for a short time before marriage and therefore felt there was little point in joining, but later in the nineteenth century women began to organise.

The Women's Protective and Provident League (WPPL) was founded in 1874, before changing its name to the Women's Trade Union League (WTUL). The WTUL disbanded in 1921 when the TUC formed the Women Workers' Group and took over much of the work of the league. Two of the most important women's organisations were the Co-operative Women's Guild, formed in 1883, and the National Federation of Women Workers, founded in 1906. The Workers Union for unskilled and semi-skilled workers, formed in 1898, was one of the few open to men and women, though women were still treated less favourably. The emphasis was always on the male wage and male work. However, its fees were low and was one of the first to have a female organiser, appointed in 1912.

The two world wars had a big impact on women's work and their involvement with unions. It was primarily the unions that objected to women workers, insisting that the jobs they took should be at lower pay and that, as soon as the war ended, women would lose their job. The government agreed to these demands. Many of the jobs undertaken were subdivided to make them easier for women, which was the justification used to pay a lower rate. Both government and unions were more interested in protecting the skilled male workers than considering how employment affected women. In the event of a pay cut, women's rates were frequently cut more than men's rates of pay. Overtime rates were often paid at time-and-a-quarter instead of the time-and-a-half that men received. Even within a union, when women worked as union organisers, they were paid less than male organisers.

One view frequently put forward by unions was that women should not press too hard for equal pay. Men's wage should be the acid test because it should be enough to support a wife and family. If both were paid an equal amount, that amount would be lower and therefore both wages would be needed in order for the family to survive. Children would suffer malnutrition because their mother had no time to feed them properly. This completely ignored the thousands of households that consisted of single women or widows trying to support their family.

It was not until the later twentieth century that women became more active in the movement and now make up the majority of members.

Travel and transport

Women working in transport sectors

Railways employed women almost from the start, though they tended to be doing tasks that were considered 'feminine'. Wives of railwaymen might work for the railway in a low-paid or sometimes unpaid capacity such as station mistress or gatekeeper. As widows they often took over the job of crossing-keeper from their deceased husbands, at a reduced wage. They were also employed in specific areas, such as cleaning in the ladies waiting room or as a stewardess to attend to female passengers.

During the First World War, women fulfilled all male roles, except train-driving, as the training period was too long. They were paid much less than men. Although they were supposed to resign their jobs when men returned after the war, in fact many women stayed on. Once refreshments began to be served on board, women became employed as barmaids, waitresses and cooks. Laundresses were needed to ensure the dining car linen was immaculate. After the war, many clerical posts were taken by women.

When the Second World War broke out, again the women were called upon to take over the men's jobs. This time the range of transport jobs increased and they were given more responsibilities, but still not equal pay. The transport unions opposed women doing men's jobs, refusing them entry to the union but, once they were allowed to become members, always insisting that male rights came first.

Women as passengers

Despite stories of attacks on women, they were not put off. As Simon Bradley wrote:

> *The arrival of the railways came to women, hardly less than men, as a liberation. To travel cheaply over long distances, alone or in company, was an opportunity open to anyone of either sex who could afford the fare. The assaults described could not have happened if single women had been too afraid to take advantage of this.*[66]

Railway stations began to be provided with waiting and refreshment rooms. At Huddersfield there were four rooms on the ground floor, a smoking room, waiting room and two further rooms upstairs. Some of these rooms were licenced and were divided by gender, then by class. The waiting rooms at Huddersfield were frequently castigated as being miserable and cold. The second-class room was 'without a fire even in this inclement season', according to one newspaper correspondent.[67]

CHAPTER FOUR

Political Life

Local government

In 1888, women were allowed to vote in county and borough council elections, but it was 1907 before they could be elected to those same councils. A local Quaker, Julia Glaisyer, was nominated in the local elections of 1910 and 1912, but lost both times to the Conservative candidate. In 1910, the secretary of the Huddersfield Women's Liberal Association (HWLA) commented that there were 'no women councillors, only two women doctors, only two women on an education committee of twenty-one, twelve women guardians out of over forty, three women on the pensions committee and three on the distress committee.'[68]

But the situation did begin to change. In 1923, the East Ward Golcar Liberal committee adopted Janet King as their candidate for the district council elections. She was a welfare superintendent at Joseph Hoyle & Sons at Longwood and was in charge of the ladies' hostel on Royal Street. The following year, Mary Blamires became the only female councillor. There were also six borough justices – including Mary Blamires, Norah Freeman and Julia Glaisyer.

In 1948, at the local election at Newsome, the Labour candidate was Alice Gardiner, who had served as mayoress when her husband was mayor in 1941-2. Her opponent was the Liberal candidate, Gertrude Jessop, a retired schoolteacher. Gertrude had also been active in local Liberal affairs for a number of years.[69]

In the event, Gertrude Jessop won the election, gaining 2,007 votes against Alice Gardiner's 1,081 votes.

Local political parties

In April 1886, the Conservative Party set-up the Primrose League Local Habitation number 1063 in Huddersfield. They established branches in the surrounding villages. It is ironic that women members did all the political work that men did: organising events, canvassing on the doorsteps, discussions with voters and so on. But they were unable to vote themselves.

By 1891, there were 2,000 members in the district. Mrs Kilner Clarke received the Order of Jubilee Star for her work for the branch with other ladies receiving the Special Service Badge.[70]

The Huddersfield Women's Liberal Association was formed in 1888. Many Liberal supporters resisted the idea of war and split from the Liberal Association in 1914. Those who previously supported Liberal candidates campaigned against them, though not actively supporting the new political movements of the working-class.

The Independent Labour Party (ILP) began in 1893, favouring the vote for all men and women. As a socialist group, they originally supported the Liberals, but eventually organised their own political association, fielding candidates in local elections. In 1933, Mary Sykes, a solicitor, was a Labour candidate for West Central Ward. She had worked for the Tenants' Defence League, the Community Club and other organisations, but placed high emphasis on the question of international peace. It was not until 1935 that Mary Sykes won a seat on the council.

Votes for women

There were a number of small groups working for female suffrage from the 1860s onwards, raising awareness and sending petitions to Parliament. Around 1874, a branch of the Manchester National Society for Women's Suffrage was formed in Huddersfield. In 1897, some suffrage groups formed the National Union of Women's Suffrage Societies (NUWSS). They primarily believed in peaceful lobbying of MPs and reasoned arguments to win their case, which was to give the vote to property-owning, middle-class women, on a par with men. Known as suffragists, not suffragettes, though the terms were often used interchangeably, Millicent Fawcett was their most famous leader. They presented petitions to parliament but with little success. The NUWSS gathered over 43,000 signatures in 1897, but in other years there were much fewer.[71]

The NUWSS supported any parliamentary candidate who advocated votes for women. Political and religious beliefs were set aside in order to promote suffrage for women. The Liberal government refused to let the matter be debated or voted on in Parliament, so many women campaigned against the Liberal Party and supported the Labour Party against the Liberals.

The Huddersfield Branch of the NUWSS was re-founded in 1904, its first president being Emily Siddon. Between 1907 and 1909, members attended mass rallies around the county, taking to the road in horse-drawn caravans to spread the message as far as possible.

Ellen (sometimes given as Helen) Studdard (née Brown) joined the NUWSS, acting as its representative to the International Woman Suffrage Alliance (IWSA) conference in Budapest in June 1913. In addition, she joined the Huddersfield Women's Liberal Association, serving on the committee and as secretary from 1900 to 1924, raising the membership to 1,410. She helped form the Yorkshire Council of Women's Liberal Association and served on its executive committee. She worked with Mrs C.W. Platts and Lydia Donkersley to organise the Huddersfield contingent of the Women's Pilgrimage. The NUWSS arranged this pilgrimage to London to demonstrate how many women wanted the vote. Florence Lockwood described in her diary how she first met the suffragettes in Huddersfield, which aroused her interest in politics and rights for women. She eschewed the riotous behaviour of the Women's Social and Political Union (WSPU), which was formed in 1903, but joined the NUWSS, for whom she made a large banner. Initially reading 'Votes for

Homes' the stitching was unpicked and the wording changed to 'Votes for Women'. This banner was carried at various rallies. A further motto, 'A New Age Demands New Responsibilities for Women', was designed but abandoned at the outbreak of the First World War.

Thousands of NUWSS members attended a rally in Hyde Park carrying their banners. According to one observer, the meeting was well organised, orderly and met with considerable sympathy from onlookers:

> *The successful carrying out of an effort on so large a scale has demonstrated ... the organising power within the National Union. From first to last some thousands of members of the National Union have taken part in the effort, hundreds of meetings and many hundreds of thousands of people have been addressed, over half a million leaflets have been distributed and over £7,800 has been collected or subscribed ... the words 'law abiding' were frequently repeated and you got what the militants had done much to obscure – the sense of responsibility dominating the great mass of women who are asking for the franchise.*[72]

In 1903, when WSPU was formed, it was led and controlled by Emmeline Pankhurst and her daughters, Christabel and Sylvia. In 1906 leading members of the WSPU spoke at a rally in Huddersfield, calling for women, especially young women, to join them and 'make their mothers' lives easier.'[73]

The WSPU primarily wanted voting rights on a par with men. Their leaders were middle-class and they expected the response to come from middle-class women. Their motto, 'Deeds, not words', troubled many women but working-class girls felt they had nothing to lose. Whether they realised that the WSPU was not advocating universal suffrage but actually excluding the very working-class girls who took action is debateable.

After the meeting, the Huddersfield WSPU was formed, their secretary being Edith Key.[74] The branch was made up largely of working-class women who could little afford to travel to London where the major rallies were held. Fundraising events were held regularly 'to defray workers election expenses'.

For a meeting in November 1907, the minutes recorded that imprisonment 'demonstrated their determination to force upon the attention of the nation the fact that women must be recognised as citizens equally with men'. Single women and widows still had to pay their taxes, without any means of voting for their own representative in Parliament. Matters relating particularly to women, such as the 1902 Midwives Act, were debated and decided on purely by men.

By 1908, Edith was writing her congratulations to members on their arrest in London. She was also asked to write a letter to those arrested, giving support from the Huddersfield branch and wishing them the health and 'womanly endurance' to complete the sentences. Edith Key died in 1937 and is buried in Edgerton Cemetery.

Eliza Thewlis took a very active part in meetings and dominated the early months of the Huddersfield branch. On 5 August 1907, a letter was sent to her asking her to 'work agreeably or resign from the Branch'. She did resign but perhaps felt she had a right to take a leading part since her daughter was responsible for bringing considerable publicity to Huddersfield.

Dora Thewlis lived in Hawthorne Terrace, Huddersfield, working in the local mill as a weaver. With both parents heavily involved in socialist matters, it is not surprising that when her mother joined the local WSPU Dora signed up too.

The first march including Huddersfield women on 13 February 1907 led to the arrest of Annie Sykes and her aunt Ellen Beever, both of whom chose 7 days in prison rather than pay a 7-shilling (35p) fine. At the next demonstration, seven women from Huddersfield were arrested, including Dora Thewlis, Elizabeth Pinnance, Ellen Brooke, Lily Hellewell and Sarah Pogson. The women were all offered a fine or prison and all chose prison.

Dora was only 17. The judge was concerned at such a young person being involved, saying she ought to be in school and suggested she go home. She refused and was returned to Holloway Gaol while the judge wrote to her parents. In response, her parents not only upheld Dora's actions but commented:

> *We find ourselves in agreement with his Honour when he says that girls of seventeen ought to be at school ... girls of Dora's age in her station of life are, in this part of Christian England, compelled by their thousands to spend ten hours per day in health-destroying factories and that the conditions and regulations under which they toil for others' gain are sanctioned by law, in the making of which women have no voice. What wonder is it if Dora should have turned a rebel and joined hands with the dauntless women who risk life and liberty in the hope that thereby justice may the sooner be conceded to their sex?*[75]

Dora, however, had had enough of prison, so when asked a second time if she would go home, she agreed. She was fêted by suffragettes but others considered her actions deplorable. She does not appear to have taken part in any further demonstrations and in 1912 she emigrated to Australia with her sister.

The WSPU continued its campaigns, suffering many times with imprisonment, forced feeding while on hunger strike, and the Prisoners (Temporary Discharge for Ill-Health) Act of 1913, often known as the Cat and Mouse Act, whereby they could be released from prison to recuperate after time on hunger strike, then re-arrested and returned to gaol. Edith Key is known to have sheltered some of these suffragette refugees from the law in the extensive attics of her home in West Parade.

When the First World War broke out, the WSPU stopped their militant actions and supported the war effort. They disbanded in 1917. The NUWSS continued taking peaceful action but also supported the war. It was renamed the National Union of Societies for Equal Citizenship, continuing until 1928 when full universal suffrage was achieved. The group then split into two groups, one of which became the Union of Townswomen's Guilds.

The Representation of the People Act 1918 gave the vote to all men, but limited it to women over the age of 30 who met certain property qualifications. In the same year, the Parliament (Qualification of Women) Act 1918 was passed, allowing women to stand for Parliament. Ten years later, the Conservative government passed the Representation of the People (Equal Franchise) Act, giving the vote to everyone over the age of 21.

CHAPTER FIVE

Community Life

Women's organisations and the Embryonic Welfare State

Mothers' Union

This was founded by Mary Sumner in 1876 to support young mothers in Winchester, and the movement spread, backed by the church. Their principal aims were moralistic but later included various aspects of social improvement, including education and health. In Huddersfield, there were branches in a number of villages around the town. In addition to helping young mothers, they held social evenings that included talks on relevant subjects and music.

There is a stained-glass window in St Mark's Church, Longwood, commemorating Mary Sumner – the only one of its kind in England.

Women's Co-operative Guild

Formed in 1883 to spread co-operation and provide women with a voice within the community, the principal organisers and members were working-class. They understood the problems of poorer, working women because that was what they were themselves. It was often by joining the Co-op and becoming a member of the guild that they began to attend lectures, to value education, learned how to manage by judiciously investing tiny amounts. They then fought, through the guild, to bring these benefits to other working families.

The Huddersfield branch began in 1892 with only twenty members,[76] meetings being held in the John Street property. By the end of the following year, there were more than a hundred members. When, in 1895, the twenty-seventh national Co-operative Union Congress was held in Huddersfield, the Women's Guild was capable of providing concerts, teas and general assistance with the arrangements.

In addition to keeping a careful eye on the treatment of their female customers, the guild developed into a campaigning organisation, not just concerned with co-operation but with suffrage and social reform. When the National Congress was held in Plymouth in 1899, two delegates from the guild (Mrs F.L. Dyson and Mrs Henry Hirst) were sent. In addition, Mrs Marshall, the Huddersfield Guild president, was a speaker, her topic being 'Women on Education Committees'.[77]

Miss C.M. Mayo was, for a short time, the editor of the local newsletter of the society, but also became a well-known speaker. She attended a meeting at Berry Brow in 1876, where she spoke about the benefits women derived from joining the Women's Guild. When she spoke in Derby in 1898, it was about a topic close to her heart, co-operative house-building, which provoked considerable discussion.

The paper she had written was published as a booklet, advocating a better standard of housing for all and saying that women should be on the management committees of Co-operative Societies, which were often in control of building schemes, because 'their special knowledge of house requirements would be most valuable'. It is not enough, she said, 'to run up houses by contract in order to get a good interest, or so that the "divi" may not fall; the convenience of the tenants, their upliftment in some cases, the saving of their time and work and their general good should be studied. A woman would make many practical suggestions that would not occur to the men.'[78]

This was part of a campaign by the Women's Guild to improve working-class housing, not just so they would be more comfortable or warmer, but to save women work.

The Charity Organisation Society (COS)

Formed in London in 1869, it believed in self-help with minimum intervention to ensure people did not become dependent on handouts. Relief, they believed, should be targeted to where it was needed, rather than spread indiscriminately. The organisation was an umbrella society with representatives from many charities in each area, giving them an oversight into activities and what help was available. They advocated careful investigation into each case before any relief was given to ensure that the system was not being abused.

In 1946, it was renamed the Family Welfare Association, becoming more involved in supporting families as a whole. It still operates today as Family Action.

Huddersfield Ladies Association for Girls

In autumn 1882, the ladies of Huddersfield got together, formed a committee and appealed for funds to help young girls. Sufficient money was raised to lease a house in Great Northern Street and Miss Rodgers was employed as matron. Such was its success that the house next-door was leased too. They discovered that girls who had already 'fallen into sin' asked for help, so temporary shelter was offered for them as lodgings in a different area until the girls could be helped in a more suitable institution.[79]

The home ran a small registry office for girls to find suitable work, classes in needlework and other subjects to help them find domestic work, as well as laundry work, partly to raise funds but also to train girls in an employable skill.

A report made after the first year revealed the need for this kind of support for girls:

> *The ignorance, recklessness and complete want of moral standards which have been revealed as existing in a large class of young women is quite appalling ... it is earnestly to be desired that ladies throughout the kingdom should realise more fully the condition of their poorer sisters and their need of protection from their enemies, from one another and from themselves.*[80]

The kind of work carried out by the ladies included teaching needlework, visiting girls who had been placed in employment, raising funds and generally overseeing the work of the hostel. Even Rev Dr Bruce made the comment that 'he never knew a combination of ladies belonging to different denominations so heartily at one in doing good work', and advocated the setting up of a Young Women's Christian Association in the town.[81]

At its height the organisation was responsible for Preventive Training Homes at Spring Street, Great Northern Street and The Woodlands, Deighton, as well as a shelter at Leeds Road, to which the girls were initially sent before assessment. They were regularly dealing with twenty to thirty girls each year who were trained, found employment and supported by the volunteers.

Friendly societies

There was a Huddersfield Female Benefit Society in 1791. Its principal rule was that members should meet on the first Wednesday of July each year for divine service. It met at the Ramsden's Arms Inn opposite the church, later moving to the White Lion on Cross Church Street, then to the Fox & Grapes on Bradford Road before returning to the White Lion. Eventually, they went to the Cambridge Temperance Hall.

However, Sarah Radcliffe was taking benefits as a widow to which she was not entitled because, said an informant, she still had a husband – in fact, she had two. She married John Armitage in 1831, then married John Radcliffe in 1852 despite Armitage still being alive. Her defence in court was that her husband, John Armitage, deserted her and their children, so she felt that a second marriage would be beneficial. The courts thought otherwise, sending her to York Castle Assizes, where she was sentenced to two months in prison.[82]

The society was still in existence in 1873 when it held its eighty-second anniversary.[83]

Female forestry

The Ancient Order of Foresters is one of the oldest friendly societies, probably starting in Yorkshire in the 1790s as the Royal Ancient Order of Foresters (RAOF). Later it split, one group continuing with the above name, the other taking the name the Ancient Order of Foresters.

Most of the groups held an annual dinner at local pubs, when the year's activities were reviewed. Court No. 1 established in 1830, held its annual meeting in 1868 at the Grey Horse Inn at Chapel Hill. Ninety members, presided over by Sister Eliza Taylor, sat down to a 'knife and fork' tea and heard that finances were favourable.[84] They met again the following year, but nothing further is known of them.

There were lodges at Linthwaite and Slaithwaite as well as Marsden, which was a very successful lodge, meeting in the Old Ram Inn from at least 1851 until 1881, when a hundred members were still gathering there.

The Meltham Lodge centred on the Swan Inn. Its meeting in 1855 referred to it being the twentieth anniversary,[85] thus being formed in 1835. The following year the female foresters took part in the celebrations at the ending of the Crimean War. There also seems to have been a group meeting at the Friendship Inn at Meltham Mills and a separate female sick club known as the Free Gardeners in Meltham.

The Holmfirth Lodge, also known as Fidelity Lodge Number Seven, met at the Rose & Crown Inn. At the 1861 meeting, one older member who had nineteen children said 'Well, then lasses, we've nobbut a day once i'th year, let's have a merry leetsome'. A leetsome means merry-making, at which there is singing and dancing. Apparently, the ladies danced and sang until nightfall when their menfolk 'conducted them safe to their several domiciles'. The following year the landlady, Mrs Bray, put on a first-rate dinner and the ladies again 'had their usual merry leetsome'. All the annual meetings of the different groups seem to have involved this kind of activity, so the ladies certainly set out to enjoy their annual 'bit of a do'.[86]

In Huddersfield the first official female court of the National Ancient Order of Foresters was the 'Sarah Ann Beaumont' Court (No. 8534), formed in 1895 and named after the wife of a member of the order. After initiating the lodge and its members, officers were elected by the ladies: Miss Mary Ramsden as chief ranger, Mrs Mary Sanderson sub-chief ranger, Mrs Annie Kaley treasurer, Mrs Annie Ward secretary, together with a number of woodwards as a committee.[87]

The British Legion Women's Section

The British Legion, which had been set-up in 1921 to help soldiers in the First World War, continued its good work in looking after soldiers' families. In 1936, the Huddersfield branch of the Women's Section was the first branch to win the standard presented by Lady Haigh, for the branch making the most progress during the year. The Huddersfield delegation to receive the standard consisted of Mesdames Beaumont, Street, Crummock, Taylor, D'Arcy and Parker.[88]

Religion

Religion permeated every aspect of life in the nineteenth century. Sundays were almost wholly given over to attending church or chapel. Children were not allowed to play, all activity had to be quiet and solemn. Though the Church of England was still influential, particularly in public office, Nonconformist chapels began to attract a greater audience because they put on more activities: Sunday schools for children and adult schools, bible classes, 'Pleasant Sunday' afternoons (or Monday afternoons for women), ladies' sewing meetings, young people's guilds, choirs, prayer meetings and sports groups. They also ran excursions to the seaside or countryside. Bazaars and sales of work helped fund their philanthropic endeavours and all were organised and run by the women in the congregation.

Different divisions

Dissenters or nonconformists consist of different groups including: Baptist, Society of Friends (Quakers) and Methodists – Primitive, New Connexion, Wesleyan, Unitarians. There were also Roman Catholics, Jews, Moravians and the Salvation Army.

Methodists allowed female class-leaders particularly for education in Sunday schools or for visiting the sick, but no ordained female preachers. The breakaway sects, such as the Primitive Methodists, made more use of women members. The Wesley Deaconess Order was formed in 1890s to train deaconesses who worked in large towns or went as missionaries overseas. They were not ordained. By 1910, women preachers were allowed but not ordained. Baptists held a similar view regarding women as unordained deaconesses.

The Society of Friends always believed in equality, with no formal hierarchy. At a meeting of the Huddersfield Bible Classes and Mutual Improvement Societies in 1896, one member 'expressed himself surprised to see ladies taking part in the association's meetings, but rejoiced to find young women's classes had been embraced by the association'. Mrs Joshua Robson, of the Friends School, Paddock, remarked that the Society of Friends had always maintained that 'The Holy Spirit had been poured upon men and women alike and women had a message of comfort, cheer and love entrusted to them, which the Church of Christ lost when it forbade woman to exercise her influence in a public manner'.[89]

The Salvation Army was founded in 1865 by William and Catherine Booth, who believed in providing practical work amongst the poor not just preaching. They also believed in equality between men and women. As well as the band for which it is generally known, the army had a strong temperance crusade, supported emigration for paupers and hired ships to help women emigrate to Australia, South Africa and Canada.

They came to Huddersfield in the 1880s, renting the old school at Outcote Bank and setting out to convert the heathen masses in their own way. In 1891, there were nine male 'soldiers' and two females: Louisa Greenwood, a captain, and Elizabeth Imrie, a lieutenant. All were quite young, the eldest being only 29.

The Rock Mission[90]

While there were many individual charities, often linked to one of the churches, few touched the depths of the poorest members of society, often considered the 'undeserving' poor. The sort of religious help offered did not reach out to these people.

In the 1870s, a number of people from different religious denominations came together to start a mission church, going out to the worst communities and trying to help them. A cottage was opened in Thomas Street in 1877 with a massive crowd attending. Three months later a lodging-house service was started each Sunday evening, eventually covering two central lodging-houses. This continued for a number of years but was stopped because of pressure from the Roman Catholic church. Many of the people in the lodging-houses were Irish, so the Catholic church had a vested interest in keeping other denominations out.

When the mission moved into new premises in 1879, their first meeting was disrupted by a rough element who rushed in, causing mayhem. Though advised to move away from the area, the mission continued, charging 1d (1/2p) for membership and getting the workers themselves to make benches to sit on. The congregation came 'on Sunday in clogs, shawls and other indications of poverty', but at least they came. Both Church of England and non-denominational congregations worked together in the mission, and the meetings were 'conducted by ladies and gentlemen from the varied branches in the town', suggesting an early acceptance of female speakers. Meetings in summer were often held outdoors, only moving indoors in poor weather.

On Christmas Day a tea was put on for the members, followed by readings and recitations. A breakfast was provided the next morning for the inmates of the lodging-house next-door. All this was paid for by mission workers, as 'the class we wished to assist have difficulty to exist, without aiding the work'. However, an offertory was provided, since many of those being helped wished to help others and donated whatever they could spare.

The mission began to have successes with a gradual improvement in the congregation 'in many cases by the spiritual influence of the women'. They instituted the usual religious groups: a band of hope, Sunday school, choir and eventually, in 1908, an adult school. There were annual excursions to local places such as Cannon Hall and Beaumont Park.

The mission's greatest impact came from the lady visitors. Mrs Mellor, Mrs Robinson, Miss Thirkill and others went to the homes of the poorest, visited the sick and offered practical help. Though little is known of the members, the Thirkill family appear on the 1891 census, living on St Andrews Road where Miss Thirkill did her visiting, so she knew the area well. They were not of the very poorest since Robert Thirkill was a teamer and the three eldest children were working. Robert's parents were living with them, his mother, Susan, being an early member of the mission from 1887 to her death in 1893.

Not all went smoothly. The church had to move on a number of occasions – from Rosemary Street to Lord Street, out to Turnbridge, before finally in 1921 amalgamating with the Queen Street Mission, which eventually morphed into the Lord Street Mission, which is still providing support for the poor and homeless today.

Religious establishments provided a respectable outlet for a woman who desired to think beyond the home. Within the church itself, women were the ones who distributed the church magazines, arranged the flowers and harvest festival contributions, and welcomed newcomers.

Girls' Friendly Society (GFS)

Women were often keen to support girls and young women, particularly those who left their homes and families to work in the towns. If they were unable to find, or lost, their job they quickly became destitute and vulnerable. The GFS was set-up in 1875 in partnership with the Church of England to help such girls. In 1890, Miss Millbank from Bedale wrote to Huddersfield Board of Guardians asking to be allowed to introduce the GFS into the workhouse, to visit the girls so that when they left it for service they might feel they had a friend. Soon after this, the GFS became established in the town, the parish church funding its first meeting room on King Street.[91]

Most of their members were in domestic service, but others were teachers, nurses, clerks, students and workers in refreshment bars, mills, factories and warehouses, all occupations that often required workers to move away from home.

CHAPTER SIX

Legal life

As a criminal

As in all societies, while part of the population was providing relief and helping the helpless, many of the helpless were helping themselves to other people's goods, providing their own kind of service to wayward men or just drowning their sorrows in whatever liquor they could get hold of. So why did women turn to crime?

Throughout much of the nineteenth century, the predominant thought (for the middle classes) was that women would be supported by their fathers, husbands or brothers. They did not, therefore, need education or training.

For the working classes the situation was different. Everyone in the house needed to contribute to family finances in some way. The slightest difficulty could result in disaster. Men being thrown out of work, turning to drink or being ill meant the family had no income. A new baby caused considerable expense and prevented the mother from working for at least a week or two.

Winifred Casey was well-known to the police.[92] She was 4 feet 10 inches, with dark-brown hair and a scar on her right hand. In 1885 she received two months in prison for stealing 4 shillings and in 1888 she and two friends, Mary Ann Dyer and Mary Clasby, robbed Jonas Wimpenny. They all had a string of previous convictions, so Winifred was sentenced to eighteen months. As well as stealing, she had previously been convicted of assault, damage, being drunk and incapable, and brawling. In 1889 she was sentenced for theft to twelve months in Armley Gaol, she was only 23. She probably spent the rest of her life in and out of prison, resorting to stealing and prostitution to obtain a precarious living and getting into brawls while drinking in the local inns.

Women who could not support themselves or their family had to go into the workhouse. There they were separated – only children under 7 were allowed to stay with their mothers. Boys and girls were split into different areas and the family rarely met up. The idea was that children could then be trained in a useful occupation, away from men and women, including their parents, who might be a bad influence.

Though women were capable of committing just the same crimes as men, they tended not to be as violent. Often they acted as lookouts or assistants to male criminals.

Prostitution

Although we feel we know what 'prostitute' means, in the nineteenth century the definition was much wider. It could be used to mean any woman who had a sexual relationship outside marriage, or a woman who lived with a man who wasn't her husband, or a girl who had an illegitimate child, or a woman who sold her body for sex.

The Contagious Diseases Acts did not involve any action against the men or condemnation of their using prostitutes, but did take drastic action against women. Police could arrest any woman they thought might be a prostitute. A woman arrested was forced to undergo highly intrusive medical checks for venereal disease. If found to have any infection, she was forcibly detained in a secure hospital for however long the courts decided or until she recovered. Although the first Act only covered a few specified naval and military towns, later Acts extended the law to cover more areas. In 1869, the Ladies National Association for the Repeal of the Contagious Diseases Acts was set-up, arguing that, rather than insisting men should have their sexual desires catered for, therefore prostitutes must be kept healthy, men should instead be forced to control themselves, respect women and follow their lead of higher morality. After many years of campaigning, the Acts were finally repealed in 1886.

Brothels

Many brothels were run in backrooms and bedrooms of inns, but some brothels were dedicated houses. In 1850, John Bayldon and Hannah Armitage were charged with keeping a brothel.[93] They lived together but weren't married. A young girl was brought up as a witness, who said she'd come to Huddersfield where she'd met Hannah, who had persuaded her to work for them. They provided board and lodgings, so long as she handed over everything she earned. Bayldon and Armitage were simply bound-over to keep the peace.

In 1880, Maria Fountain was charged with keeping a brothel. The police watched the house for a number of nights, either questioning or recognising the men, as they stated in court that many of them were married. Maria had been keeping the brothel for at least twelve years, always in the same area. The police did comment that some brothels were more orderly than others and Maria's house was 'the house which the most respectable people in the town who went to such places went to'. Some of her neighbours even gave her a good character as she was kind to them, though others did complain. The defence solicitor agreed that the events had taken place, he had no defence to those but pointed out that the 'house of its class was respectably conducted'. The law against these houses must be upheld, he said, but would closing one improve the situation or just push the clientele into worse houses? The magistrates eventually fined both accused £5 each plus costs, and Maria Fountain further small sums for keeping brothels open on the nights proved.[94]

Not all prostitutes had accommodation for their pursuits but were quite happy to improvise. When the police stopped John Chappel, a cab-driver whose cab was being driven furiously in town at one o'clock in the morning, Sergeant White remonstrated with Chappel, but he wasn't the one driving. A woman was holding the reins. She was drunk and had been whipping up the horses all the way along King Street, New Street and High Street. Inside the cab was a prostitute with her client. Chappell was fined 5 shillings (25p) with costs.[95]

In prison

By the mid-nineteenth century, female prisoners could expect to be looked after by female warders, often known as correctional officers. Wakefield is the nearest prison to Huddersfield, but police stations had their cells, earlier known as 'the lock-up'. The constables looked after the prisoners, with female searchers to look after women. On a less formal note, the wife of the nearest police officer could be called upon to act as chaperone.

In 1901, the Association of Lady Visitors was formed to bring together all women who visited female prisoners, giving help and support, and to set a model of good behaviour. Male prisoners did not get this help until much later, but in 1944 the two groups amalgamated to become the National Association of Prison Visitors.

The wardresses in prison had to be a minimum of 24 years old, maximum age 35, single or widowed with no dependents. Pay started at around £55 a year, rising to over £150 for a matron of a large prison. Lady superintendents were placed in charge of all female staff and convicts, but under a male governor. In 1911, better training was established with an entrance exam, including basic reading, writing and arithmetic.

During and after the Second World War, women were encouraged to go into the prison service. The career was 'opened up to eligible girls or widows', with the advantages of an attractive uniform and pay.[96]

The prisons included evening classes, concerts and lectures and free accommodation for warders, though they had the option of living-out if they wished. Pay could be anything between 15 shillings (75p) up to £4 10s (£4.50) per week for a prison matron.

For many women, this must have offered some security of income and a good standard of living, though the accommodation when living-in was not specifically built, often just being an end cell converted to give a little extra comfort. Night duty meant sleeping in the prison undertaking night duties with no extra pay. Men could be married and continue their job, so they could have a family life and a break from the bleakness of prison. Women who lived-in had no family life and no social life since the doors were locked at night. Once married they generally had to leave the service, though there were exceptions if staff recruitment was difficult.

Women's legal identity

A woman only remained an individual if she were single or widowed. Younger women 'belonged' to their father, married women to their husband, so the law was wary of intervening between a man and his property.

In 1852, Ann Kaye stole a dress from Mrs Bake who ran her own business as a corset-maker. Mrs Bake was unable to do anything about the theft. Only her husband, Thomas, was able to prosecute Ann because the dress was legally his property.[97]

Violence against women was commonplace, moderated principally by the neighbours. Women had little legal redress against their husbands. Violence could be for any perceived neglect or simply because the husband felt like hitting someone. If she ran away, the police, when they found her, legally had to return her to her husband.

Despite the fact that education was not widespread before 1870, women seem to have understood very quickly just what the Matrimonial Causes Act of 1857 meant for them. It came into effect in January 1858 and by February, the first case was before the magistrates in Huddersfield. The newspapers did not provide any personal details, just that a married woman applied 'for an order under the recent Divorce Act to protect her earnings and property from her husband and his creditors, he having deserted her'. He'd actually deserted her six years previously, leaving her to support herself and her family yet vulnerable at any time to his returning and taking any furniture, possessions or money she'd earned. Once the order was granted, he could take nothing.[98]

It was not always easy for women to instigate any court proceedings because of lack of money. Alice Jackson suffered considerable abuse from her husband. In 1890 she left him, taking their 9-year-old daughter with her. Though he was living with another woman, he sent for Alice to return. She did go to see him and he punched her in the face, dragged her to the cellar, tried to throttle her and threatened to 'stick' her. Though she merely asked the court for him to be bound-over to keep the peace, they added a one-month prison sentence to the request.[99]

Alice was unable to instigate divorce proceedings then as she had no money. It was two years later before she and her friends managed to save sufficient money to ask for a divorce, which was granted, Alice gaining custody of their child. Harry Jackson was ordered to pay 2 shillings (10p) a week maintenance for the little girl.[100]

It was not just the wife who was interested in ensuring that her assets were secure. Where the husband had absconded, it was in the court's interest to grant the separation so that if the husband returned, he could not take any money his wife had accumulated and disappear again, leaving the family to be supported by the poor rates (a local charge on householders to support the poor).

In 1923, women as well as men could petition for divorce on the grounds of adultery. Grounds for divorce were widened in 1937, adding cruelty (including habitual drunkenness), desertion and insanity, but it was still considered that men could chastise their wives.

Florence England died in 1949. She'd previously spent three weeks in hospital before being discharged. At home she saw her own doctor, Dr Willis, who gave her sleeping tablets. Her husband, Harry England, was instructed to give her one tablet each evening. However, she also saw Dr Aspinall and he gave her some pheno-barbiturates. The two boxes were kept on top of the wardrobe.

On 24 February, Harry took her some tea but she was asleep. After lunch he called Dr Willis, who found Florence in a coma and sent her to the Infirmary. A neighbour, Nellie Pogson, promptly informed PC Campbell that she thought Harry had been beating his wife. When asked by Campbell, Harry said yes and produced a light cane stick. He explained that his wife had been sitting by the fire in the living room the previous evening and he'd asked her to make him some tea. Eventually she'd struggled into the kitchen, where she fell over on her side. He took her back to the living room settee and said, 'If you don't shape up I'll give you some cane like I do John.' Then he lost his temper and caned her four or five times. Each time she told him he was 'rotten to the core'. Later he calmed down and regretted it.

Dr Margaret Parbrook, house surgeon, said that Florence had had a number of epileptic attacks in the hospital, but some might have been due to the drugs given to her.

When the inquest concluded on 17 March, an open verdict was recorded. Death had been due to pneumonia following an excessive dose of barbiturates. There was no evidence to show how they'd been taken or if anyone had given them to her. The jury's only comment about the situation was that the 'doctor had told the husband to be firm with her and keep her about her duties in the house'. There was no condemnation of his caning her at all.[101]

As law enforcers

Female searchers

When women were taken into custody, they had to be searched. Initially this was done informally by the wife or widow of one of the police officers, but by the mid-nineteenth century, female searchers were employed. Their duties included escorting female prisoners to court and generally supervising and chaperoning them while in the police cells. By 1900, they were usually referred to as police matrons.

In 1863, the Huddersfield Improvement Commissioners decided that as well as living rent-free in the police house, the police superintendent should 'find a searcher for female prisoners'.[102]

In 1869, Mary Shaw, a greengrocer, was accused of passing base coin (which her husband, Jonathan, had made). When Mary was taken to the police station, she was searched by 'the female searcher', though nothing was found. Later Mary turned informer, since she wasn't actually married to Jonathan. She was sentenced to one month in prison. Jonathan was sentenced to eighteen months. On his release, he returned to live with Mary, now using her maiden name of Schofield, together with their five children.[103]

Other searchers included Rose Ann Fox in 1869-70, Mary Ann Hoyle in 1873, Mrs Rowley in 1886, Mrs Renshaw in 1888, and Sarah Jowett in 1891, who received the salary of 12 shillings (60p) per week. Mrs Jowett worked for the police for at least ten years. She didn't just search female prisoners but also laid out bodies and inspected them for signs of injury. In 1894, an unknown woman leapt from Somerset Bridge. Sarah dealt with the body, later stating in court that the body was fairly well-nourished. 'The deceased was clean and tidy and was fairly well-dressed. There was just a slight bruise on the left temple, but there was no mark of violence on the body.'[104]

Though many Victorians considered anything even slightly gruesome to be unsuitable for a woman, this did not seem to apply to working-class women. When James Bottomley was killed on the railway line, Sarah laid out the body and gave evidence of seeing a 'large wound, about 3 inches long, on the left side of the head and which penetrated to the brain, there were bruises on the right shoulder, elbow and thigh'.[105]

Lady police assistants

Edith Hoyle was Huddersfield's first female police assistant between 1915 and 1917.[106] Lily Mary Allen was 'lady police assistant' between 1918 and 1923.[107] After Miss Allen left, there seems to be no reference to women police as such until

(*Above*) WR Asylum, Stanley Royd, Wakefield.

(*Below*) Co-operative Restaurant, Buxton Road, c1910.

Sixty Years' Success.

WHELPTON'S PURIFYING PILLS.

TRADE MARK (REGISTERED)

For INDIGESTION, HEADACHE, BILIOUSNESS, CONSITPATION.

INVALUABLE FOR LADIES.

Sold by all Chemists at $7\frac{1}{2}d.$, $1/1\frac{1}{2}d.$, and 2/9; or free by post for 8, 14, or 33 Stamps from G. WHELPTON AND SON, 3, CRANE COURT, FLEET ST., E.C.

(0155)

(*Above*) Advertisement for Whelpton's Pills.

(*Below*) New Hey Road, workers housing.

(*Above*) Martha and Irene (standing) Shaw and Sarah Singleton.

(*Right*) Sheila Dixon (on the right).

(*Below*) Oakes Board School.

Map of Castlegate 1893.

(*Above*) Crosland Moor Workhouse.

(*Below*) Trinity Nursing Home.

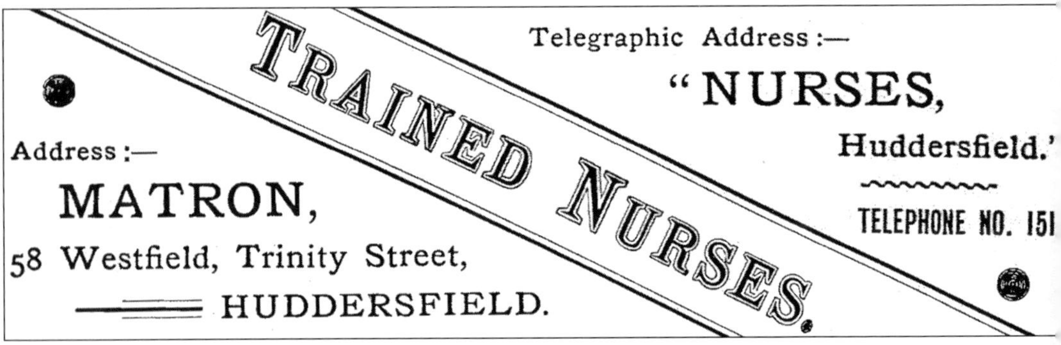

Telegraphic Address:—
"NURSES, Huddersfield."
TELEPHONE NO. 151

TRAINED NURSES

Address:—
MATRON,
58 Westfield, Trinity Street,
HUDDERSFIELD.

(*Above*) Advertisement for Nurses.

(*Left*) Old Royal Infirmary, New North Road.

(*Below*) Crosland Moor Infections Ward.

(*Above*) NSPA on their way to London, 1939.

(*Below*) Great Western Inn, Marsden.

MRS. J. HELLEWELL CARTER'S
VULCANIZED
India Rubber and Gutta Percha
MANUFACTURES.

AIR AND WATERPROOF FABRICS OF EVERY DESCRIPTION.

CART & WAGGON COVERS,
ROOFING AND HAIR FELTS.

India Rubber Valves, Washers, Sheet Rubber, Hose Piping, Gas Tubing, Machine Belting, &c.

Any article made to order for Mechanical, Nautical, Surgical, Travelling, Sporting, Manufacturing, Miscellaneous, and Agricultural purposes.

4, BUXTON ROAD, HUDDERSFIELD.

(*Above*) Advertisement: Mrs Hellowell Carter.

(*Below*) Acre Mill, Lindley.

EDUCATIONAL COMMITTEE.
Top Row: H. H. Goodyear, S. Lockwood, G. Wilson, and C. H. Daniel.
Bottom Row: Mrs. Marshall, J. S. Armitage, and R. Ledger.

(*Above*) Co-operative Educational Committee.

(*Below*) Railway Station, St George's Square.

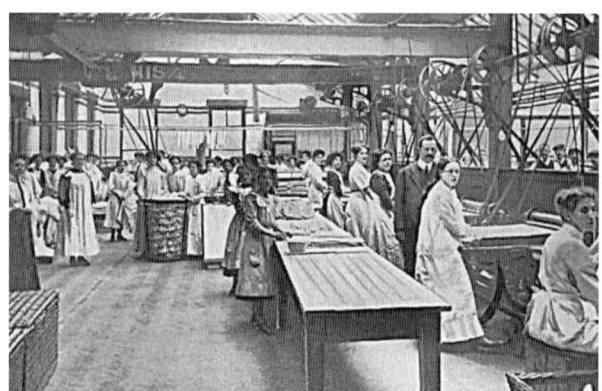

(*Above*) Hawthorne Terrace.

(*Left*) Co-operative Laundry c1910.

Kirkburton Police station built 1868.

(*Above*) St Peter's Parish Church.

(*Below*) Town Hall.

(*Above*) Lion Arcade Buildings.

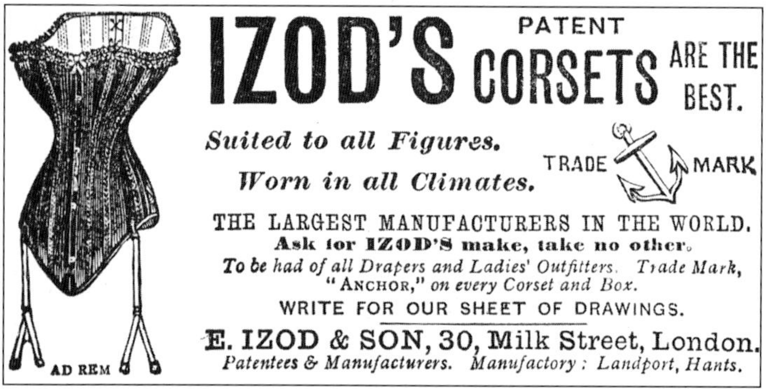

(*Left*) Izod's Corsets.

IZOD'S PATENT **CORSETS** ARE THE BEST.

Suited to all Figures.
Worn in all Climates. TRADE MARK

THE LARGEST MANUFACTURERS IN THE WORLD.
Ask for IZOD'S make, take no other.
To be had of all Drapers and Ladies' Outfitters. Trade Mark, "ANCHOR," on every Corset and Box.
WRITE FOR OUR SHEET OF DRAWINGS.

E. IZOD & SON, 30, Milk Street, London.
Patentees & Manufacturers. Manufactory: Landport, Hants.

Library and Art Gallery.

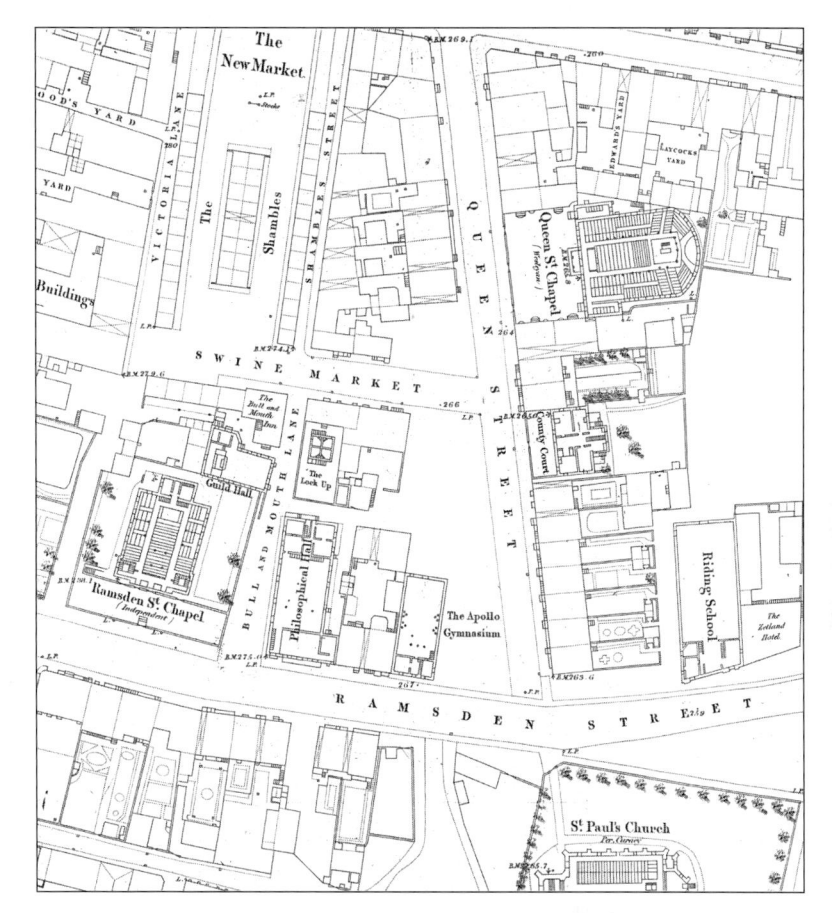

(*Right*) Map showing Philosophical Hall 1851.

(*Below*) The Sisters Moore.

THE SISTERS MOORE.

Miss DECIMA MOORE Madame BERTHA MOORE Miss EVA MOORE Miss JESSIE MOORE

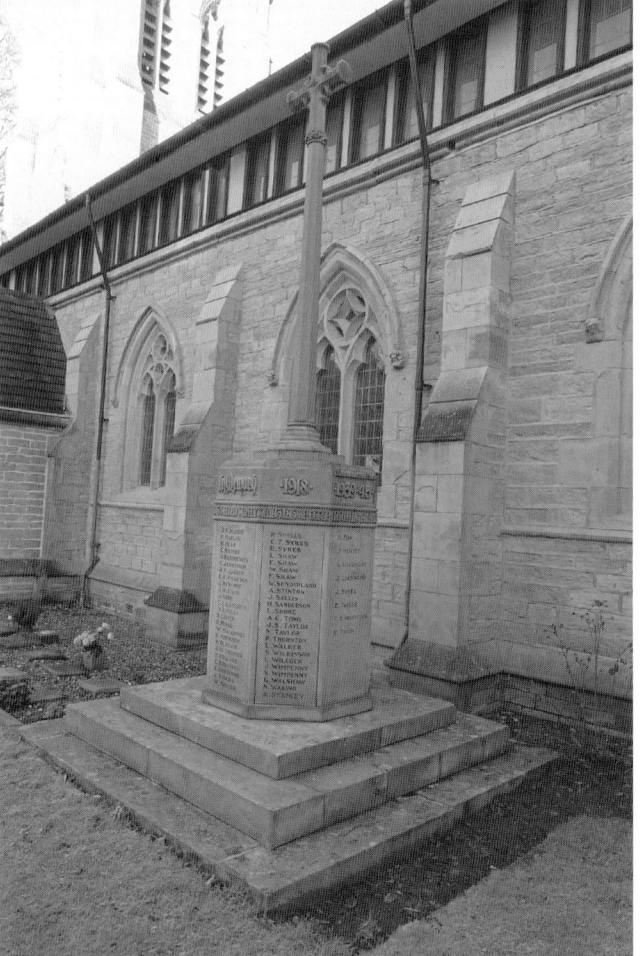

(*Above*) Fallen Heroes statue.

(*Left*) Armitage Bridge memorial, A Stanley.

(*Above*) Wellington Mills.

(*Right*) Advertisement for Sewing Machines.

INTELLIGIBLE—COMPREHENSIVE—RELIABLE.

THE DICTIONARY OF
MEDICAL & SURGICAL KNOWLEDGE.

A Practical Guide, in Health and Disease,

FOR FAMILIES, EMIGRANTS & COLONISTS.

TWENTY-FIFTH THOUSAND.

With One Hundred and Forty Illustrations.

Complete in One Volume, handsomely half-bound, marbled edges, **5s.;** or in Two Vols., cloth, **2s. 6d.** each.

The GLOBE says:—"An excellent work for the use of heads of families. . . It is not intended to supersede the services of medical men, but it will help mothers and nurses to know when professional advice is really required."

The CHRISTIAN UNION says:—One of the best handbooks on this subject for popular use. It is concise, simple in character, comprehensive in its subjects explicit in its remedies, and perfectly reliable. The author has adopted simple language and simple remedies, in order to make the work useful in every household."

The CHURCH STANDARD says:—"A handbook to which heads of families may safely appeal in the hour of emergency when no duly qualified practitioner is within reach. To emigrants and colonists such a *vade mecum* as is here presented must assume a priceless value."

Crown 8vo, 232 pages, cloth, 1s. 6d.; or in leather, 3s.

FAMILY RECORDS:

A Ruled Book for Systematically Registering the Dates of
INTERESTING EVENTS, BIRTHS, MARRIAGES DEATHS, VISITS, ETC.,
IN THE FAMILY AND THE SOCIAL CIRCLE.
Also an Account of the Household Expenditure.

"Most certainly a book to recommend, and, if carefully kept and handed down from generation to generation, would become a most valuable possession. Fancy what entertaining reading such a book would be if only our great-grandmother had had it; and why should we not think of our own great-grandchildren? Such a book carefully filled and put aside may amuse future generations, and 'keep our memory green' long after the hand that wrote it has mouldered in the dust."—*Lady's Pictorial.*

London : HOULSTON & SONS, Paternoster Square, E.C.

For Families, Emigrants and Colonists.

1944, when Dorothy Haigh joined after five years in the fire service. Dorothy had to leave in 1946 when she had her first baby. It is probable that 'police matrons' were employed to deal with female prisoners instead of 'police assistants'. During the Second World War, their status increased as the range of jobs they were allowed to tackle expanded.

In 1919, the Police Federation was set-up as a staff association for all police. Women police were only allowed to join the federation in 1948. By 1948, there were only three police women in Huddersfield – Doreen Cartwright, Phyllis Beverley and Hilda Tagg.[108]

Solicitors

Women were barred from all the professions, including the legal profession, until the Sex Disqualification (Removal) Act came into force in 1919.

Mary Sykes

Mary was one of the first women in England to register articles with the Law Society, working in her father's firm of Armitage, Sykes & Hinchcliffe. She worked alongside Edgar Sheard who, in his autobiography, remembered their time together:

> *At this time we articled clerks had rooms on the third floor of 1 Westgate and Miss Sykes' room adjoined the one occupied by Harry Longbottom and myself ... we took tea together in Miss Sykes room every afternoon. I look back on those tea parties with great pleasure. There was interesting conversation between four persons, all with different backgrounds ... Miss Sykes was much admired and loved by us all.*[109]

Unfortunately, her father died in 1921, but she completed articles and became a fully qualified solicitor at the end of 1922. She continued working for the firm until 1930, when she branched out on her own. But that was not the end of her public life. In 1935, she became the first female Labour candidate to be elected to the town council, becoming the first woman alderman in 1937 and Huddersfield's first woman mayor in 1945. Around a thousand women queued up in Ramsden Street just to see the lady mayor, which they described as a 'fitting tribute to the part women played during the war'.[110]

Magistrates

One of the first female magistrates was Emily Siddon. Appointed by the lord chancellor, Miss Siddon was only the second lady magistrate in the country, but it was 'principally for the certification of lunacy and will be held by Miss Siddon as long as she retains the chairmanship of the Guardians'.

The newspaper went on to say 'that the honour is well deserved will be conceded on all hands and the numerous admirers of Miss Siddon will rejoice at this further recognition of her public spiritedness'.[111]

Other female borough magistrates in 1924 included Mrs Julia Robson Glaisyer and Miss Mary Irving

Probation officers

In 1907, the Probation of Offenders Act allowed the use of workers who became official officers of the court. After the First World War, the probation service became more formal, being brought under full state-control in 1938. At this time it also became compulsory for female officers to be in charge of female probationers.

In 1948, 28-year-old Naomi Wallace succeeded Mrs Clarkson as a female probation officer in Huddersfield. Naomi had served in the Auxiliary Territorial Service (ATS) during the war and held a social science diploma from Oxford.[112]

Early the following year she was involved in a case of three girls who had formed a shoplifting gang. They admitted sixteen offences and also being involved with a fourth girl in stealing from a chemist's shop. They truanted regularly from school and refused to co-operate with Naomi, who was their probation officer. The magistrate sentenced the two 10-year-olds to an approved school, the leader to a further two years' probation and the youngest to be taken into care.[113]

Jury service

The Sex Disqualification Act of 1919 removed the bar to women serving on juries, though the judge could insist on a single-sex (i.e. male) jury in cases where he deemed this appropriate. Legal counsel could also ask for any juror to be removed without having to give any reason.

Isabella Easingwood was charged with attempting to obtain money by false pretences, for which she'd been convicted in the local magistrates court and sentenced to twelve months in prison. She then appeared in the Quarter Sessions court on a charge of shoplifting and stealing a lady's fur. She objected to the three women jurors, saying she did not want any woman to try her. The judge upheld her objection and the women had to leave. The case continued with an all-male jury who found her guilty.[114]

CHAPTER SEVEN

Social Life

Shopping

In 1854, the Lion Arcade was opened in St George's Square. Behind its magnificent façade were brass-framed, glass-fronted showrooms for a range of shops, including booksellers, china and glass shops and Miss Radcliffe's crochet parlour, which included a ladies' room 'very elegantly fitted up'. Bands played in the gallery, there was a promenade, with a fountain, the full length of the building. Mrs Hirst had her cigar and fancy goods shop next to the register office for servants.[115]

If the Lion Arcade was for the well-off, the new market hall, opened in 1880, was patronised by 'middling' folk. The side of the building contained glass-fronted shops selling meat, game and fish. Inside were seventy-two stalls, with gas lights. A stone-carved clock-tower rose over a hundred feet (30 metres) above. But prices would have been considerably lower than anything found in the Lion Arcade.[116]

There was a surprising number of women who ran shops. In Cross Church Street, Ellen Bowker opened a glass, china and earthenware shop, not far from the baby linen and ladies underclothing establishments of Mary Kendall, and Martha Berry and Hannah Swift. The shops of Mrs Burton, millinery, Alice Burton, straw hat-maker, Widow Bayldon, toy-dealer, and Miss Susan Mellor, a music teacher were all to be found on that same street.

Eleanor Bottomley inherited a coachbuilders yard in Kirkgate, which she ran for many years, expanding the yard and winning at least one tender for work in repairing damaged tram cars. In 1880, she had acquired enough capital to buy out the business of George Oldfield Donkersley of Beast Market when his business failed.[117]

In the late nineteenth century, department stores began to develop. Aquilla Rushworth opened a store called 'Huddersfield Bazaar' in 1875 selling fancy goods and toys, gradually expanding their range to china, glass, cutlery, leather and household items. In 1926, they started a cash on delivery system, enabling them to sell goods via the Post Office. In the Second World War, clothes sold became more practical, including slacks (trousers) for ARP duties done by women. Dungarees, pen torches, and anti-splinter nets (these were stuck to the window with water to prevent shards of glass flying around during air-raids) also found a place in the store. Blackout material was sold too.[118]

Mourning

Fabric warehouses, milliners, dressmakers, hatters, glovers and shoemakers always had a good stock of black materials to ensure that demand could be met. A widow was expected to wear black for at least a year. Many remained in black for the rest of their lives, like Queen Victoria. Mourning for other members of the family varied between one year for close relatives to a few months for more distant relatives. After the set period of mourning, soft colours such as grey or lilac would be worn for a while before moving back to brighter colours.

Mourning also required the purchase of mourning cards – announcements of the death with details of the interment, printed on elaborate cards with engravings of angels or ivy and always black-edged. Stationery would also be black-edged during mourning. Special mourning jewellery, often made of Whitby jet, was also worn. Even servants had to be provided with black armbands.

Christmas

Prince Albert introduced many of the aspects we know today, helped by the increase in mass production factories that brought cheaper goods to a wider range of people. The publication by Charles Dickens of *A Christmas Carol* in 1843 spread a universal idea of what Christmas was about across the country.

Beef or goose had been the traditional meat, but gradually turkey became cheaper and more available, though the poor had little different from their normal fare. Some of our most popular carols come from this era: *See Amid the Winters' Snow* was written in 1851; *O Little Town of Bethlehem* in 1868; *Away in a Manger* in 1883. Christmas cards began in the 1840s, too. The halfpenny post in 1870 brought their sending within the reach of most of the working population.

All this, of course, required considerable preparation both in the home and in the shops. Each year the local newspapers reported on the best shops to visit for provisions. In 1890 a whole paragraph was given to Mrs T.W. Sidebottom's confectionery shop on Buxton Road. She was ready to make all kinds of cakes to order, including a Christmas cake. For gifts, recommendation was given to Mrs A. Marshall's shop in New Street, which sold drawing and painting requisites. 'Scarcely a more interesting gift could be made to a young person with artistic proclivities,' the newspaper said.[119]

An article entitled *Christmas Preparations in Huddersfield* described a range of shops that were gearing up to provide everything the Christmas shopper could want. All the shop windows were decorated and lit-up after dark 'by means of the electric light', their displays and shelves packed to capacity. All the fabric and dressmaking shops were stocked with the latest fashions – even the mourning department of Denham's was restocked over Christmas. Items for the home could be bought as presents or to make the home look better for guests.[120]

In 1900, there was an annual treat for the aged and the poor in the parish church school, where 150 people were given a Christmas dinner. The infirmary had decorated trees in many of the wards, patients were given presents with a turkey dinner at noon. All this provided by a 'committee of ladies who annually exert themselves for the welfare of the patients'. The sanatorium too was decorated with trees, garlands and filled stockings for the children. At the workhouse at Crosland Moor, the guardians took on the job of providing and serving a Christmas lunch, which included beef, pork, mutton and vegetables, followed by plum pudding. Deanhouse Workhouse inmates were entertained in the same way. The Post Office was inundated with Christmas cards and the staff had to work up to eleven o'clock on Christmas Eve. The 'services of the young lady telephone operators, nine in number ... were requisitioned', to ensure the post went out.[121]

Many firms sent out catalogues for their own goods. By the end of the nineteenth century, home shopping from a store catalogue, such as Empire Stores and Kays Catalogue, was widespread. Women used the catalogues to purchase items for the house because they could pay for them week by week. Some ran the catalogues themselves as a way of producing a tiny income.

Fashion

In 1842, the *London Illustrated News* became the first newspaper to carry images of its news stories. Ladies in Huddersfield were now able to order items from London and be sure they were at the height of fashion.

It was in the 1870s that the bustle became popular, along with constricting bodices that required corsets to be laced tightly to show off minute waists. The corset was a laced bodice, often referred to as 'stays', which covered the upper body. It ended with a slight flare to spread out over the hips and the tops of the thighs. Stiffened with bone or sometimes thin steel it compressed the chest, restricted breathing, displaced internal organs such as the liver, caused poor blood circulation and, sometimes, a prolapsed uterus. In Edwardian times, stays developed a rigid front that pushed the body forwards so that the pelvis was pushed backwards. This caused less injury to the internal organs, but much more to the back.

As the fashion changed to more flowing dresses, the corset began to fall from favour. This was helped during the war years when women were asked to stop wearing corsets in order to free up metal for munitions. Girdles became popular in the 1950s. Though often referred to as corsets, these were effectively deep belts that could be worn to hold in the stomach without doing too much damage.

The new century brought in frilly blouses, lace collars and the popularity of skirts with blouses and massive hats held in place with long hat pins. Ostrich feathers, silk flowers and other decorations were all the rage.

All this became pared down with the advent of war, when fabric was scarce and women were out at work, needing more practical clothes. Hemlines rose to meet the long strings of pearls that were slung round the neck during the Roaring Twenties.

By 1936, the fashion for shorter skirts for 'day frocks' became the rage. The International Council of Women, at their conference in London, pointed out that fashion shops had an impact on older women too, but could do much to support them. By the age of 30, women began to fear growing old. They suffered a lack of money because the wages were low, so they couldn't save for old age but had to try and find a job. There was a lack of companionship and a lack of job opportunities, so the council called on shops, especially clothing shops, to employ older women on the grounds that women want to be served by someone of a similar age to themselves, someone who understood the problems.[122]

The Second World War not only influenced the length of skirt but included the general style that was admissible and also rationing for clothes, with each garment needing a set number of coupons before purchase.

Unlike food coupons, clothing coupons could be spent at any shop, but the government was concerned with the type of clothing and footwear that would be in the shops. They planned special designs that reduced the amount of material used and made the best use of the raw material. It now became 'honourable for civilians to be seen in clothes which are not so smart'. They would be seen as bearing: 'a share in war if we too are battle-stained. By making do, you are helping towards another gun or tank.'[123]

In 1942, the government introduced the utility scheme, designing clothes to use the minimum amount of material with little embellishment. 'Make do and mend' became bywords. Classes were provided, showing how to cut patterns to best advantage and how to mend clothes. Many department stores offered a mending service, which included mending socks and underwear as well as patching jacket elbows and turning collars. It was only in 1947 when the 'New Look' was launched by Christian Dior that fashion started to become more extravagant again, but many shops still had the older utility clothes in stock, which they needed to get rid of before bringing in the new spring fashions. Some shops had tremendous bargains. Coats that had cost £16 plus eighteen coupons could now be had for 30 shillings (£1.77) plus only nine coupons. Costumes or suits were the same price, where previously they had cost £5 plus eighteen coupons. Unfortunately, few of these massive bargains were to be had in Huddersfield, where the majority of shops simply had their normal January sales, with perhaps a little more off the prices than usual. Where the reductions were large, the queues started at 7 am and the items were sold within fifteen minutes. The queues, however, remained orderly no matter how great the bargain.[124]

After the Second World War, smart women wore a costume or suit with skirt and jacket. Almost all women wore a hat. Working women wore basic skirt and blouse with a pinafore over the top to keep the clothes clean.

Whatever fashion dictated, clothes had to be made. The top of the hierarchy had their dresses privately made, either by one of their servants or by a dressmaker. Slightly lower in the scale was the seamstress, who did basic sewing, often working for a dressmaker. They would also make alterations to clothes that were handed down from mistress to servant or adult to child. The poorer classes made their own clothes or bought second-hand.

Arts

Artists

Annie Wood was born in 1854. She studied at the Mechanics' Institute and the Huddersfield School of Art. In 1873, Annie's examination results show that she passed in geometry, but received grade Excellent in freehand drawing, perspective and model drawing.[125]

She attended the School of Art in South Kensington in London before returning to Huddersfield, where she was appointed art mistress at Fartown Grammar School, remaining there until 1914. One of the founder members of the Huddersfield Art Society, she regularly exhibited her paintings. At the society's first art exhibition in 1890, the critique said that:

> *Miss Annie Wood's three drawings, in which portions of the interiors of well-known cathedrals are very charmingly reproduced possess an irresistible attraction to many. They represent careful, conscientious work and are really very artistic productions.*[126]

She also exhibited with the Yorkshire Union of Arts and in Leeds and Whitby. She was a member of St John's Church, Birkby, and designed the lettered panels of the ten commandments for it. She died on 15 March 1915.

Music

The Huddersfield Choral Society[127]

The Huddersfield Choral Society was formed in 1836. Although it was run by men, females were admitted from the start. The performances they gave were purely private, not on the public stage, but they still expected a high standard of singing and commitment to the group. Some of the earliest female soloists were Miss A. Milnes, Miss Sykes and Mrs Peace. There were actually two ladies called Mrs Peace in the society, Mrs James Peace and Mrs Lister Peace.

It was 1842 before the group finally gave its first public performance, principal singers being chosen from among the members. Mrs Sunderland was the principal treble (soprano) and Miss Crosland the alto. In later years, the principals tended to be paid professionals in order to attract a wider audience, with support from the members of the choir.

In 1872, funds were low so a special concert was held in Greenhead Park to raise money. One of their members, Sarah Jane Mosely, a music teacher, also put on a concert with some of her own pupils and raised money for the society, thus enabling them to continue. When the town hall was opened in 1881, the choral society sang at the event and continued to put on their performances in the Town Hall from then on.

A ladies' committee was set-up, partly because finances were again low and action was needed, but it also reflected the way in which women were becoming much more active generally. In 1911, Madam England became the first lady on the society's musical committee. She was re-elected every three years until she decided to resign in 1929. Mrs Irving Kay joined the committee in 1923 and Madam Lottie Beaumont in 1928.

There were a number of glee and madrigal clubs in Huddersfield. The Huddersfield Glee and Madrigal Society was formed in 1875. It was a mixed choir from the start. They entered their first competition in Manchester and won it.

Due to falling interest and finances, the society had to disband in 1884, but it was reformed later that year. The group then went on to win a competition in Liverpool in 1886 and became joint winners at the Welsh Eisteddfod in 1887. The mixed voice choir shared a prize of £200. The choir celebrated its centenary in 1975 but later changed its name to the Huddersfield Singers.

Other glee and madrigal groups were formed in Almondbury and Marsden.

Mrs Sunderland

Susannah or Susan Sykes was born in Brighouse in 1819. She was helped by a local blacksmith who first trained her voice.

Though her natural talent shone through, her early efforts were of 'a very rude and uncultivated character'.[128]

However, after she sang at a meeting of the Ramsden Arms Glee Club, one of the earliest musical societies in Huddersfield, they engaged her for a full season at 5 shillings (25p) a night. Before long, she was earning £5 a night for her singing. By 1835, she'd become the principal treble (soprano) at St Paul's Church, and continued with them for a further seventeen years.[129]

In 1836, she became a member of the Huddersfield Choral Society and continued to sing with them for most of the rest of her career. She earned her living through her singing, travelling not just around the West Riding but throughout the country, including London. In 1838, she married Henry Sunderland, taking his name on stage as well as in private life. They had six children.

In 1856, Mrs Sunderland was at the centre of a major disruption between Huddersfield music supporters and Bradford. When St George's Hall in Bradford was opened in 1853, Mrs Sunderland had sung *If God Be For Us*, which was considered a difficult song and not one of the greats. However, she performed it well.[130]

Three years later, in 1856, Bradford had another concert at which Susannah was booked to appear. However, when she asked to be given a part in *Elijah* or the *Messiah*, she was informed that nothing was available in those as all the parts had been allocated to other principals. The only song she was given was *If God Be For Us* again, and this she accepted. However, that song was later removed from the programme in order to shorten the event.

At this Mrs Sunderland dug in her heels and informed them that if she wasn't allowed to perform her part in the oratorio, she would decline to attend the concert at all. After some acrimonious correspondence the committee wrote that if she sang at the hall she must do so 'when and where we, the committee, think most suitable'.

Further letters followed and Mr Smith then wrote to *Leeds Mercury* implying that Mrs Sunderland was being petty. She promptly sent the newspaper extracts from all the correspondence, showing that she was the innocent party. Public opinion sided with the singer.

A festival in her honour was then arranged in Huddersfield. Two of the ladies who accompanied Mrs Sunderland, Miss Whitham and Miss Freeman, were Huddersfield ladies. The event was considered a resounding success and a worthy response to Bradford's unsportsmanlike behaviour.[131]

Mrs Sunderland decided to retire at the age of 45. Huddersfield put on a concert to mark the occasion 'after her brilliant career as a public singer of nearly thirty years duration'. Thousands packed the streets outside the Town Hall and traffic was stopped so that those not able to attend the concert could hear some of the music.[132]

On the occasion of her golden wedding anniversary, a concert was staged in Brighouse in her honour, the proceeds of which were used to set-up a regular competition, initially as a vocal solo competition to be held in Huddersfield. Later other classes were added, including instrumentalists and choral.[133]

The first of these Mrs Sunderland competitions was held in April 1889. There were thirty-seven competitors including twenty-seven lady singers. Mrs Sunderland presented the prizes. The festival has continued to take place every year since, except in 1940, during the Second World War. Mrs Sunderland died in 1905.

Charlotte Elizabeth Beaumont

Charlotte was born in 1888 in Golcar, daughter of a dyer. She was known throughout her career as Lottie Beaumont, despite marrying Harold Hallas in 1915. She joined the Huddersfield Choral Society in 1909, eventually being voted onto the committee, serving twenty-one years.

In November 1916, she went to London with the local glee and madrigal society to sing Mendelssohn's *Elijah* in Westminster Abbey for the wounded soldiers. The newspaper comments that they would have lost at least two days' pay to do this, quite a sacrifice in those days.[134]

In 1917, a musical group from Huddersfield, including Lottie Beaumont (contralto), Constance Wilkinson (soprano), Elsie Beanland (violinist) and Haydn Sandwell (accompanist), went to France to entertain the troops. They worked hard, giving two or three concerts each day in makeshift theatres, sometimes with long journeys between. At one camp, the room was so packed the men were hanging on the roof railings and sitting on the roof crossbeams. Backdrops were old army blankets and lighting was provided by oil lamps. Concerts were given in hospitals, garages, aeroplane hangars, to soldiers about to go to the Front or just returned, to those wounded and to those looking after them, to British, Australian and Canadian troops. They even managed to visit the army veterinary camp to see how horses were cared for. The singers suffered from the cold and wind, getting sore throats from having to sing over the roar of the guns, but managed to provide twenty-seven concerts in fourteen days, entertaining 25,000 people.[135]

She continued her musical career, conducting the Huddersfield Choral Society and singing in concerts around the country. But in 1949 she decided to retire. Her last concert was a performance with the Huddersfield Choral Society. She said that she 'wished to retire while her singing powers were still good ... the older ones should make way for the younger generation'.[136]

Miss Frances Mary Hefford Cocking was born in 1882 in Kirkheaton, Huddersfield. She became a music teacher and composer, publishing various kinds of works: nocturnes, variations, lullabies, and a sonata in three movements. The list of music shows how talented she was. Some of her music survives in the West Yorkshire Archives, including an arrangement of music to a West Riding Folk Song *Jenny Jog*, which goes through the week's work in a house. It was arranged for a ladies choir. She was a member of the Society of Women Musicians (SWM) from its foundation in 1911 until 1920. In 1914, Frances joined the Society of British Composers. This had been founded in 1905, but it was 1914 before women were allowed to join. In 1938, when a carnival was held to raise funds for the Royal

Infirmary, Frances was the one who organised a choir as part of the entertainment.[137] Frances died in 1955.

Writers

The Huddersfield Authors' Circle was formed in the 1930s as a self-help group. Since one of its rules is that members must have had work published, many members wrote pieces for local newspapers, even if only for the letters columns. The circle still continues today.

Hazel Wheeler was born in 1927 in Huddersfield, brought up in a village shop run by her parents. She wrote diaries from the age of 14, cataloguing her experiences at school, during the war and her married life. Details included major events, such as the outbreak of war, but also memories of tiny events in her life or things she saw, what the weather was like and the prices of items in the shops. The diaries were later written up into a number of books, describing life and the people around Huddersfield. She joined Huddersfield Authors' Circle in 1950, continuing to write about her own experiences, but also about those of her mother. She died in 2009 in Kent, but the funeral service was held in Huddersfield, where she is buried.

Phyllis Kelway was born in 1906 in Langport, Somerset. At the age of 25, she decided to come north, settling in Huddersfield, to make her name as a writer. She began writing about gardening topics, progressing to various aspects of nature and becoming a well-respected naturalist, widely published in many magazines. She used her own photographs as illustrations, which were considered to be of the same excellent quality as her writings. Phyllis not only observed nature but also conducted research, including studying rats, mice and snakes. She became the first person to breed harvest mice successfully in captivity.

Her death was unexpected and probably related to her work. She and two friends, Mary Sykes and Ada Dunch, had set-up home together on a smallholding in Almondbury that they called Arkholme. Here she spent her time watching the animals and birds about which she wrote, as well as looking after any injured or abandoned creatures. She was taken ill and died within a few hours of being seen by her doctor. At the inquest, Dr Guest, who did the post-mortem, suggested that she had died of 'respiratory failure due to gas gangrene septicaemia'. This could have been caused by a scratch becoming infected by bacteria in the soil, but no definite answer could be found.[138]

Sports

Some sports, such as golf, tennis and swimming, seem to have been open to women with little criticism and, in fact, with considerable support. Other sports were definitely male preserves, which women were condemned for playing as being unladylike or endangering the species.

Cricket

Women playing cricket had generally been within the family or at boarding school. Men's teams had a ladies' committee responsible for providing teas and arranging fundraising or social events, by which women supported the men's clubs, who acknowledged that without the women, the clubs would have difficulty functioning. It gave the women chance to socialise, meet young men under supervised circumstances and ensured that the behaviour of the men was rather better than found at football or rugby matches, which were primarily attended by men.

Towards the end of the nineteenth century, women began playing cricket in a more organised way. The Women's Cricket Association (WCA) was founded in 1926, run by women for women.

The Holme Valley was a particular hot spot for cricket. In 1929, when the Holmfirth Cricket Club needed to raise funds, their secretary, Miss Tinker, organised matches amongst the wives of the players. This was so successful that the Holmbridge Club followed suit and they organised a competition. Teams came from local mills, churches or local men's teams with women's sections. Eleven teams entered. The league was played for charity and their first match was well-attended by many 'people who had never seen a cricket match of any kind (but) went to this match to see how the ladies would shape with bat and ball'. They raised £5 for charity.[139]

The matches continued, attended by an average of 2,000 people, and all went well until the match of 30 June. The score was close – 36 to the 'Reckless Set' and 37 to the 'Holmbridge Revellers'. The losers insisted that they had also scored 37 and stormed the scorers' hut, heckling and shouting. The total was allowed to stand, but after further complaints it was decided to have a rematch.[140]

By July the reporter conceded that the standard of playing was improving. 'If they continue to progress with the rapidity with which they have done up to present, some of the male players in the Holme Valley will have to be giving up their laurels to their fair vanquishers.' The final match in the league took place in August between 'St John's' and 'Lower Mills', Lower Mills winning by two runs. The winners won a silver teapot each, the losers were given silver spoons.[141]

The Yorkshire Women's Cricket Federation (YWCF), formed in 1931, was set-up by men and all committee members were men. This helped promote the men's matches, they could hire out the grounds to the women's teams or take the gate profits for the general benefit of the club. The WCA was largely controlled by educated, middle-class women who had learned cricket in their schools. The federation attracted mainly working-class girls and women, often belonging to workplace teams.

Support for ladies' cricket was particularly strong in this area and Huddersfield teams took part in many of the games. Women's cricket seems to have had its heyday in the 1930s, attracting large crowds. In 1930, a ladies' team from Messrs Robson's of Dalton played a match against the Cowcliffe Ladies. The Robson's team were in 'modern' dress – white shirt and white trousers – while the Cowcliffe team wore crinolines and frilly bonnets. The weather was raining and the ground muddy. Not surprisingly, the dresses got soaked, clung to the ladies' legs and, whenever the players tried to run, they were more likely to fall over.

Miss Scott, secretary to the Cowcliffe Ladies, arranged the match to prove that 'to play cricket, ladies must wear clothes that allowed freedom of movement'. The reporter agreed that crinolines were not suitable and stated that: 'really, there was nothing shocking about the Dalton ladies in their white flannels and crickets shirts. They looked extremely neat and business-like and as cricketers (or should it be cricketesses?) they showed distinct promise.'[142]

In 1933 the team, which had been known as Holme Valley, moved from its original base in Thongsbridge to Paddock, where it was hoped the easier access would provide a larger audience and therefore bigger 'gates'. The name was changed to Huddersfield and they entered the Yorkshire Inter-City and Town League. As only one club from each district could play in the league, no other team in the area could enter.

Fixtures were arranged with Brighouse, Halifax, Dewsbury and Savile, Bradford, Sowerby Bridge, Dingley and Keighley. Each game lasted twenty to thirty overs. Two of the players, Miss L. Hill and Miss R.W. Humphries, gained county recognition.[143]

Football

The earliest known ladies' match was in 1881 in Scotland against a team of English ladies. The British Ladies' Football team started in 1895. The secretary, Miss Nettie Honeyball, said: 'We ladies have too long borne the degradation of presumed inferiority to the other sex ... If men can play football, so can women ... It's a delightful sport and every member is enthusiastic about it.'[144]

Women's football grew during the First World War when women came together to work in factories. Their matches were well-attended, partly because of the novelty, partly because of the charities they supported. In Huddersfield, the principal football team was the Atalanta Club, formed in 1920 by a group of middle-class women 'to provide games for the women of Huddersfield, to foster a sporting spirit, and a love of honour among its members'. The chairman was Constance M. Waller of Birkby, who also became the first female newspaper reporter to work for a provincial paper. In 1921, the ladies formed a Gold team and a Blue team, who played against each other, trying to learn how to play the game mostly by watching some of the men's matches. In January of that year, they had a practice match at Sandhouse that was described as their 'best day' so far. Blue team won 2 – 1.

The Huddersfield league secretary undertook to train the girls, deciding that they needed to practise football two nights a week and spend two nights a week on physical training. 'This only goes to prove how necessary was the Atalanta Club. Its object is to provide the games and exercise that every girl has a right to but which were previously very difficult to obtain.'[145]

In March, their first 'proper' match was arranged for Good Friday. A lady from Bath took exception to the timing, complaining that women should be in the home or in church. Constance Waller wrote back refuting the suggestion. 'We are coming into a new age physically. When all girls realise the great pleasure that playing football and cricket gives, there will be less girls spending their time idly walking the streets or reading sticky novels.'[146]

The game took place at Leeds Road, with more than 15,000 spectators to see Atalanta beat the Bath Ladies 1 – 0. The winning team was made up of Ethel Lee, Hilda Clarke, Minnie Kenworthy, Lily Mitchell, Rhoda Wilkinson, Constance Waller, Mrs L. Barraclough, Alice Stanley and Misses Edgely, Steele and Broadhead. Miss Broadhead scored the goal.

During the war, and for some years afterwards, women throughout the country continued to play football. They had no grounds of their own since few women or women's teams could command the capital needed to buy a ground. Instead they played on the men's football grounds, continuing to draw large crowds whenever they played. On 5 December 1921, the Football Association gave their opinion that football was not a suitable sport for females. It told all affiliated clubs to refuse the ladies the use of their grounds. This effectively stopped women's football, though some clubs did continue. The English Ladies Football Association (ELFA) was formed in 1921,

Huddersfield's Mrs Barraclough becoming vice-president. Mrs Barraclough, a newly-elected vice-president and captain of the Huddersfield Atalanta, said she thought that before long practically all the women's clubs in the country would be in the association. Asked how many clubs there were in England, she replied, 'It is impossible to tell, but there must be 150. Lancashire and Yorkshire are swarming with clubs, and quite a lot are being formed in the London district.'[147]

A match was played at Grimsby between a team drawn from various Yorkshire clubs and the local Grimsby teams, again for a nominated charity. Miss Whitwam and Miss Mitchell (reserve) represented Huddersfield.[148]

The next ELFA match was in Plymouth, this time Mrs Barraclough was listed as from Huddersfield Atalanta, Miss Whitwam as 'Huddersfield' and Miss Mitchell as from Huddersfield Town. This suggests there may have been a number of ladies' football clubs in the town at that time.[149] Most could only continue as amateurs, playing on second-rate grounds.

Entertainment

Libraries and the printed word

Class affected how women's leisure time was used, including what she read. However, reading was often seen as an immoral waste of time or was proscribed by father or husband as being 'unsuitable'. Free public libraries were not widespread. Churches may have a Sunday school library that stocked books of a religious nature and could be borrowed by the teachers to read to the children. The cost of belonging to subscription libraries meant that it was only the middle-class and above who could afford to join.

In 1880, nine years after the Huddersfield Improvement Act 1871 had allowed the setting up of a local library, the town council mooted the question of a free public library. The ratepayers, who would have to pay increased rates for it, voted against the suggestion. The free public library was finally opened in 1898 in honour of the Queen's diamond jubilee celebrations, with the newsroom and reading rooms being well-attended. It was decided that ladies were not restricted to their own room, but could go into the general room to read the papers.[150]

Eventually the library outgrew its first rooms and a new site was acquired in 1934. The new library building opened in 1940, including a ladies' room, though there was no 'official' opening then because of the war. The art gallery opened in 1943.

Huddersfield Industrial Society set-up the first free public reading room in 1893, with a lending library the following year. Like many others, once the free council-owned library became established, there was no need for any others and, in 1931, the Industrial Society library closed.

Some books were considered *risqué* or even banished from the house. *Tess of the d'Urbervilles* had for its heroine a woman who has an illegitimate child, commits murder and is then hanged, yet is depicted, and recognised by many, as being the victim of Victorian society. *The New Machiavelli* by H.G. Wells showed the unsatisfactory nature of marriage from the point of view of a woman.

Almost all the libraries gave access to newspapers in their reading rooms. The national newspapers came up from London, but there were also local ones such as the *Leeds Mercury,* the *Leeds Times,* the *Huddersfield Chronicle & West Yorkshire Advertiser* (from 1850) and the *Huddersfield & Holmfirth Examiner* (from 1851 but dropped the *& Holmfirth* in 1853).

As early as 1861, the *Manchester Times* had its 'Ladies Column' providing domestically focussed items such as a useful 'receipt' or recipe for dyeing hair:

> *Moisten the hair first with a solution of silver in nitric acid and then with a weak solution of sulphuret of ammonia. This is instantaneous in its effect; it is to be observed that it also stains the skin.*[151]

The ladies' column of the *Penny Illustrated Paper* published in London had correspondence pages where ladies could write in and ask questions. Some included a more political note, such as a report from the House of Commons describing the ladies' gallery, then the view of the House with its 'rows of bald gentlemen' and which party sat where.[152]

Magazines began to proliferate from 1850 onwards. One of the earliest was Samuel Beeton's *The Englishwoman's Domestic Magazine* (1852-1881), aimed specifically at the middle-class. It had a supplement written by his wife, Margaret. She collected these into her famous book *Mrs Beeton's Book of Household Management*. She also wrote the *Book of Needlework*, which included fabric with a pattern printed on it or a pattern transfer to iron onto bought fabric.

The *Girl's Own Paper* was published by the Religious Tract Society to ensure girls, between the ages of 13 and 23, had the right sort of guidance in their lives. It included romantic fiction and household hints. The *Ladies' Treasury*, started in 1857, included illustrations and articles on history, geography, literature, education and fine art as well as the usual domestic items. The editor, Eliza Warren, gave advice that was suitable for households with just one servant and thrift was encouraged, suggesting that the readership was more lower-middle-class or skilled working-class.

There seem to be no magazines aimed specifically at working-class women, possibly because they lacked purchasing power and had little leisure time. Newspapers were read by men in pubs, clubbing together to buy one paper to be passed round or read aloud by those able to read. Sunday school and elementary schools provided the only place where books were encountered, but these could not be taken home. As literacy improved, cheap serialised prints of sensational stories were produced, sold at 1d (1/2p) each. They became known as 'penny dreadfuls' and were very popular. Though not aimed at women, they were cheap enough to appear in some working-class households.

By the end of the century, many more magazines were published. *The Lady* began in 1885 for middle-class women who needed a genteel job. The major women's magazines began after the turn of the century: *Woman's Weekly* in 1911, *Woman's Own* in 1931, and *Woman* in 1937.

Other entertainment became available in 1922 when the BBC radio service began, but it was 1946 before *Woman's Hour*, the first programme specifically for women, began. Politics, women's place in the world and in society and other issues were discussed, with less emphasis on home-making.

Theatres and cinemas

People always find means of entertaining themselves and having a little fun to brighten their lives. Drink frequently plays a part, so entertainment often began in inns and beerhouses. Everyone could join in singing and beating the rhythm on the tables. The majority of the participants were men, with just a few women. It was only later that the music halls developed into variety theatres to which men and women could go.

One famous theatre in Huddersfield was Rowley's Theatre of Varieties. The usual programmes were light entertainment, such as songs, conjuring and pantomimes. In 1890, a pantomime called *The Prince of Paddock*, written by Rowley himself and incorporating many local references, was put on. The leading role was taken by Pattie Rowley, who was a great hit singing such songs as *Castlegate Militia* and *Fair Daisy of Damside*. References were made to the Huddersfield football team, but unfortunately just what the references were is not stated by the newspaper.[153]

Probably one of the best-known theatres in Huddersfield was the Theatre Royal. The first premises were built before Victoria became queen and were known as the Philosophical Hall. Benches were rearranged for a variety of purposes, such as plays and music.[154]

In 1856, it was the scene of a festival held in honour of Mrs Sunderland. The building continued to be known by many as the Philosophical Hall, though others began to call it the Theatre Royal. In 1876, it was as the Theatre Royal that it was given a licence to stage plays, but in 1880 it burnt down. The following year it re-opened and continued in that form until 1961, when it was demolished.

The Gilbert and Sullivan operas, written between 1871 and 1896 were very popular because they mocked Victorian society. Combined with beautiful music and witty verses, they spawned Gilbert and Sullivan societies in almost every town.

Huddersfield Amateur Operatic Society began in 1896, with a production of *Iolanthe* in 1897 at Theatre Royal. This was a big success, followed by *Yeoman of the Guard* the next year. Miss Winifred Boyle was, apparently, a clever actress, with 'a true and natural interpretation of the part [of Dame Carruthers], she used her rich contralto voice with great musicianly skill, both in her solo and concerted music'.[155]

The next year, *Patience* was put on, in which both Winifred Boyle and Honora Walker were lauded for their singing and acting ability. Over the years other operettas were performed: *Merrie England*, *The Vagabond King*, *The Desert Song* and *Tom Jones* – all very popular in the early part of the twentieth century. The group is now known as the Huddersfield Musical Theatre Society.

The Original Opera Company, now known as the Huddersfield Light Opera Company, was formed with a view to producing something different, particularly something that might appeal to a younger audience. The comic opera *Les Cloches De Corneville* or the *Chimes of Normandy*, was their first effort and was put on at the Theatre Royal on 6 April in 1912.

During the First World War, they produced a new opera, called *The Pink Elephant,* which was a cheerful, optimistic show designed to raise spirits. On New Year's Day they gave a matinée performance at which soldiers from the local war hospitals attended. It was a popular way of raising funds. Subscribers paid all the costs, and profits of over £70 were shared amongst various local war charities.[156]

Drama too had its supporters. As early as 1853, the Huddersfield and Halifax Amateur Dramatic societies gave performances in the theatre in Ramsden Street. The Huddersfield company put on *Lady of Lyons*. All the main parts were taken by professional actors, with locals supporting. Their production in 1875 raised the sum of £42 5s (£42.25), which was donated to the infirmary.[157]

The thespians began playing the small theatres, deciding to go for good, literary plays rather than just the 'popular' ones, though their first play, at the Temperance Hall, was a play entitled *Don*, a comedy by Rudolf Besier (who also wrote *The Barretts of Wimpole Street*), put on in October 1920. The main female parts were taken by Kate Montgomery, Letitia Beaumont, Mary A. Wibberley, Gladys Mann and Violet Broadbent. Later that year was G.B. Shaw's *Mrs Warren's Profession*. The play is about the madam of a brothel, a former prostitute, and her daughter. Though the daughter chooses the moral high ground and rejects her mother, the play was considered very controversial at the time. In 1922, it was Ibsen's *The Doll's House* which, again, showed they were prepared to tackle some contentious themes as this is essentially about a woman's dissatisfaction with her role as housewife. Rather appropriately their production in 1939 was *Arms and the Man.*

Many amateur theatricals were associated with churches, townswomen's guilds, co-operative societies and other community groups. The stages for these were the church hall, or small, more private, venues. For many of the women involved, this was a more acceptable way of appearing on stage, rather than the public events in the larger theatres.

Bertha Moore

Bertha Moore was born in Sussex and studied music at the Royal Academy. Her sisters, Decima, Eva and Jessie, were all famous actresses. In 1887, she came to Huddersfield to sing at one of the Huddersfield subscription concerts. Her 'reception was a most enthusiastic one. This lady possesses a soprano voice of exquisite purity and sweetness ...' Not surprisingly, she was asked to return the following year and, in fact, sang at the concerts for many years, as well as singing with the choral society.[158]

In 1888, just a year after her first professional visit, she married Frank Huth, a member of a prominent Huddersfield family. Bertha continued her career, using her maiden name prefaced with 'Madame' instead of 'Miss'. As well as keeping up her stage career, Bertha took an active part in civil life in Huddersfield. When she did so, she was always referred to as Mrs Frank Huth. She helped organise a concert, along with her mother-in-law and a number of other ladies. This was put on at the Armoury by the Compton Comedy Company, specifically for poor 'men, women and children'. All the inmates of the workhouse were able to attend, and everyone was presented with an orange and a bun on leaving.[159]

Bertha died in 1940 at Maidenhead, aged 77.

Holidays

Railways provided fast transport, which was relatively cheap and enabled many more people to journey further. The 'middling sort' of people began to go to the seaside: to Blackpool, Scarborough, Bridlington and Skegness. Sunday schools, friendly societies or works all arranged for a day at the seaside.

In 1871, the Bank Holidays Act provided the impetus for everyone to have the day as a holiday. Agricultural shows at Honley, Emley and Holmfirth were also big attractions for a day out. The Great Yorkshire Show did not then have a permanent site, but Huddersfield was host in August 1888, with more than 40,000 visitors at Longley Park. The show came to Huddersfield again in 1931, when it was held at Dalton.[160]

Easter 1893 had good weather, encouraging people to go out and enjoy it. There were many special bookings on trains as well as the ordinary timetabled ones. Places visited included Southport, Blackpool, Scarborough, London and Belle Vue, which was a large zoo and amusement park near Manchester. Afternoon trips also went to Littleborough and Hebden Bridge.[161]

Eventually, Saturday became a half-day off and some white-collar workers were given a week's annual leave. Mills found it more convenient to close the whole mill for a full week.

This pattern continued until well after the Second World War. Sheila Dixon remembered how, in the 1940s, her mum and dad both did extra work at home in the evenings for the local fireworks factory making cases for fireworks to save enough to afford a holiday at Mrs Robinson's lodging-house in Bridlington. Every day her mother would consult Mrs Robinson, go shopping for the food and Mrs Robinson would cook it for them for tea.[162]

The first holiday camp was set-up in 1906, but it was after Billy Butlin developed his camp at Skegness in 1936 that things began to change. Most catered for only 200 to 300 people, Butlin's catered for 2,000. He came up with the idea of red coats staff to help entertain the holidaymakers. By the time the Second World War ended, he had built camps at Filey and Pwllheli, both of which were within easy reach for the people of Huddersfield. Conducted motor-coach tours were also very popular, especially trips to Ireland. Closer to home, Blackpool was, as ever, a favourite place for day trips.[163]

The Holiday Pay Act of 1938 provided for one week's paid holiday for working-class employees. By the 1950s, two weeks were common.

CHAPTER EIGHT

Impact of War

The South African (Boer) War

There were two South African wars. The first, between 1880 and 1881, involved the Dutch settlers, or Boers, who left the Cape area and trekked across Africa. They objected to the British policy of treating white and black people in the Cape area equally.

In 1899 in the Transvaal, Britain became involved over the voting rights of the Uitlanders who were mostly British miners. In October 1899, the second South African War broke out. The newspapers became filled with stories of the sieges, and later relief, of Ladysmith, Mafeking and Kimberley.

The second South African War involved more men and therefore more families were affected. It also lasted longer and became notorious, not only for the sieges, but also for the policy of bringing civilians, particularly women and children, into one area, partly to ensure they were safely out of the warzone and partly to ensure they were not able to assist the soldiers. This idea of 'concentration camps' had already been used successfully by both Spain in Cuba and America in the Philippines, but caused considerable difficulties for the British in South Africa. The newspapers were full of stories of hardship. After the Ladies Commission investigation headed by Emily Hobhouse, the government was forced to take action and things improved.

In May 1900, the people living in the St Andrew's Road area found out what it was like to be under a bombardment of shellfire. An outlying shed belonging to Read, Holliday & Sons had blown up, scattering debris across a huge range. Windows were smashed as far as Beast Market, Northgate and Byram Street in the centre of Huddersfield. Mrs Betty Broadbent, a 60-year-old widow, had all the windows in her house broken as well as those in the house she owned nearby. Mrs Horn, also a widow in the area, was hit on the leg and arm with debris and suffered similar damage to her property. Mrs Sheard was so shocked she had to be taken to her son's house in Wakefield Road and refused to go back to her home.[164]

In Huddersfield, the ladies went into action in their own way. In December 1899 a ladies' committee was formed 'for the despatch of comforts to the West Riding troops at the Front'. Funds were raised to send food parcels to the men fighting in Africa, particularly the volunteers from Huddersfield. In December 1900, letters were received from Lance-Corporal J. Walker and T.H. Holden, thanking them for the 'warm clothing and tobacco' and glad that 'we have so many friends in Huddersfield'.[165]

The 'Fallen Heroes' statue in Greenhead Park was set-up in 1905 and became a focus of annual memorial services until the First World War memorial was completed in 1924.

The First World War

Women's support in terms of fundraising, taking over men's jobs and through their work in the hospitals, both at home and abroad, was invaluable.

Sister Ada Stanley trained as a nurse in the Royal Infirmary. She was part of the Territorial Force Nursing Service and was sent on active service to the Dardanelles in July 1915, going out on the hospital ship HMS *Northland*. Later she developed dysentery and was taken to the military hospital at Netley, near Southampton, where she died. Her body was returned to Huddersfield for burial in Armitage Bridge. Soldiers from the local regiment bore the coffin and her name appears on the war memorial there.[166]

Nurse Evelyn Faulder joined the First Aid Nursing Yeomanry (FANY), which provided ambulance support to the Red Cross. She served in the warzone between 1916 and 1919, eventually earning the Military Medal for 'gallantry and conspicuous devotion to duty' when an ammunition dump was hit by enemy bombs and Evelyn was one of those who went to rescue the wounded.[167]

Voluntary Aid Detachment (VAD)

After the South African War, the government realised there were insufficient nurses to cope. Women were encouraged to learn basic skills from the Red Cross to provide extra nursing support to the Territorial Forces Medical Service. When war broke out, many VADs volunteered for service. Initially the women worked only in Britain, but soon they were needed at the Front too, where they worked alongside fully qualified nurses, drove ambulances or acted as hospital cooks, clerks and cleaners. Many of the nurses in the auxiliary hospitals in Huddersfield were VADs. Red Cross Awards were later made to nurses M. Story and Jeannie Strickland, who were both VAD nurses at the Huddersfield War Hospital.

Huddersfield War Hospital at Royds Hall

A campaign was started for Huddersfield to provide its own war hospital. Within five weeks of the campaign starting, £21,000 had been raised and, by October 1915, the mayoress, Mary Blamires, was asked to perform the ceremony of opening the hospital – a great compliment to the women of Huddersfield. They were the organisational force behind the fundraising, providing equipment and accessories such as bed linen, etc. More than 24,000 articles had been supplied to the hospital before it opened and the women then embarked on producing uniforms for the nurses and pillows, with cases, to rest wounded limbs on.

Fundraising

A great effort was needed to help the families left behind, to deal with wounded soldiers and provide the extras needed by fighting soldiers. Requests included sewing, knitting, visiting, office work, messengers, houses for convalescents, nurses, gifts of all kinds such as money, red flannel for bed jackets and wool for socks. Funds were needed to buy materials for women to make up into whatever was required. The deputy mayoress, Doris Scott Thomson, headed this appeal, but many women formed their own groups and held knitting sessions to produce socks or coffee mornings to raise the funds.

These organisational skills were a product of the groups and societies women and girls already belonged to – YWCA, Girl Guides, Mother's Union, as well as the women's suffrage movement.

War relief fund

The Huddersfield & District Women's Committee was started by Mrs Kilner Clarke for the wounded soldiers. All the districts around Huddersfield were linked in, via the central depot on Ramsden Street. Links were also made to the war hospitals, local army corps and to the central London organisation.

In the receiving room, goods such as cloth, flannel, wool for knitting, cigarettes, stationery and so on, were sorted and stored. Items could be requisitioned and sent directly to wherever needed. Women everywhere were involved in producing socks, small muslin bags filled with sphagnum moss for dressings at the hospital, mosquito nets and even anti-vermin pants and vests, which were made with material soaked in carbolic acid.[168]

Women at work

With so many men away, the country could not function unless women took over jobs that had always been considered 'men's jobs'. In 1915, the Women's War Register became available for women to register in the job centre for 'war work', primarily in munitions. Picric acid, known as Lyddite, had been produced in

Huddersfield during the Boer War and by December 1915 even more was being made.

Edith Staley worked in the TNT (trinitrotoluene) department of a local chemical factory. There she worked down a pit, but this made her feel sick. After four weeks sick leave, she moved into the benzol and toluol department, which did not affect her as much.

On 23 December 1917, a spanner was dropped 'from 30 feet' and hit Edith on the head, causing concussion. She was treated at the works, but later saw her own doctor, Dr Ratray. Another doctor, Dr Baldwin, also saw her at some point and said she had jaundice. Eventually, she was admitted to the Royal Infirmary where she died. Cause of death was given as toxic jaundice that had considerably reduced the size of her liver. The inquest verdict was accidental death from TNT poisoning accelerated by the blow on the head.[169]

Other work

Since around 8,000 men had left Huddersfield to join the forces, many machines had to be left idle until women could be trained to take over their jobs. There was an influx of women workers into munitions work of all kinds. They came mainly from north and east Yorkshire and the East Midlands, needing accommodation and transport. The Huddersfield Women's Hostel was regularly packed with women coming in search of employment, and with visiting wives of wounded soldiers.

The winter of 1917 was severe. A massive snowstorm and blizzard struck the area, causing problems for the post girls who were delivering the mail. One confessed to 'shedding tears at the work load', while another had caused great concern because of her late return. She explained that she'd 'had to go breast-high in snow in places'. But all the girls went out on their second deliveries, despite being given the option not to go.[170]

New laws

The new situation called for new laws and new means of imposing them. Huddersfield's first lady police assistant was Edith Hoyle, appointed in April 1915. Under the Children's Act, she toured the theatres and music halls in the area, ensuring that children who performed there were out of the venues by nine o'clock and attended school during the day.

Commanding officers would often write to Edith asking about the conduct of a soldier's wife. Edith would visit the women and have a chat. The separation allowance was not much and often money had to be obtained 'by other means', presumably prostitution. Sometimes she would find the house in darkness and the children crying upstairs, or find a pram parked outside a pub. Then she would go in and ensure the mother went home.[171]

Assisting would-be deserters was an offence. Ada King suffered because her son-in-law deserted from the army in April 1917. On 11 May, the police arrived to search the house, which they did, despite being told that he'd not been there for five weeks. He was found in a cupboard. Ada was prosecuted for harbouring the man, her defence being that he'd arrived at midnight and 'she'd had to suffer for her daughter'. Ada was sentenced to seven days in prison.[172]

In 1917, the Women's Army Auxiliary Service (WAAS) was formed and many women joined-up. There were no officers, just controllers and administrators. There were four units: clerical, mechanical, cookery and miscellaneous. Apart from the mechanical section, the jobs reflected the views of what was suitable for women to do. They had khaki uniforms, but still received less pay than men, even if doing the same job. They supported men in the army camps, mainly in England but also on the continent, by running the canteens, working in administration, repairing motor vehicles and keeping the camps clean.

In 1918, four young women went absent without leave from their army camp. Captain Moore, Huddersfield Police, received information that all four of them were on a train but refusing to pay their fare. Moore sent for Nellie Broadbent, daughter of his superintendent and a sergeant at the camp, who identified the four girls. At the magistrates court the next day, they all pleaded guilty but explained their behaviour as being annoyed because they'd been at the camp for three months, had not been treated well and having been refused leave when they'd requested it. All were locked up while awaiting an escort back to camp.[173]

Social effects

The Huddersfield branch of the National Council for Combatting Venereal Disease held a meeting in the Town Hall. The speakers commented that the subject was the responsibility of both men and women, but the blame was targeted at 'flappers', young women who supposedly flung themselves at anyone in uniform, but needed both sympathy and support from private clinics. Bad housing, lack of teaching about the subject of sexual hygiene, and the 'intemperance' of the girls were contributing factors. There were over seventy meetings planned for the area, so the subject was obviously of great concern.[174]

The National Union of Women Workers discussed the subject and heard a report from Mary Irving about the 'patrol sub-committee', which oversaw women patrolling the streets. They had already had some success in redirecting some girls, but also gained much insight into their situation. Huddersfield decided to set-up special clinics at the infirmary to help those suffering the disease, and appointed a lady doctor.

Transport

The tramways, particularly, were hit hard as many of the men they employed had been reservists and were the first to be called-up. By July, the solution appeared in the form of 'four attractive young ladies learning the duties of tram conducting.'[175]

By December 1915, even more responsibilities were given to tram conductors. They were now serving on through-routes such as between Honley and Sheepridge. 'The result is they have often to collect fares on crowded cars, a by no means enviable position for a woman to be placed in. Still they are not at all dismayed and get through their work with wonderful patience, a virtue in which they seem to excel.' It seems that many of the male passengers were also very helpful to the new conductresses. One 'gallantly rendering what service he could by ringing the bell while the conductress collected the fares'.[176]

Food shortages

The effects of the German blockade caused serious concern that Britain would not be able to feed itself if the war continued. People were asked to reduce their consumption of bread. Different flours were used and additives, such as peas or beans, helped to make the grain go further. The bread had to include at least five per cent flour from rye, oats or barley.

As starvation became a greater threat, Huddersfield Food Control Committee commandeered margarine from shops in the district, a ration card had to be produced for purchases. Everyone had to register with a butcher to claim their meat rations: 5oz (0.142 kg) meat (including bone) per person per week. Teashops and cafés could not sell crumpets, muffins or any other 'fancy' breads; no cakes with more than fifteen per cent sugar (normally this would be around thirty per cent), and no more than 2oz (0.056 kg) cake or bread per customer.

National kitchens

The government set-up national kitchens where large amounts of basic food could be produced and sold more or less at cost. In Huddersfield the first national kitchen was opened in Aspley in July 1918. There was nowhere to sit so meals had to be taken away. A full meal costing around 8d (4p) might include a Cornish pasty, vegetables, rice and a pudding such as jam roll or ginger pudding and custard.

After the war

The Representation of the Peoples Act 1918 had almost trebled the number of parliamentary voters and, for the local government voting, women outnumbered men for the first time. The first general election after this extension of the franchise took place in December 1918.

Many men returned physically injured or mentally disturbed. At home, too, life had changed. Women had tasted the freedom of working, earning a wage, being independent. Others found their lifestyle diminished as the breadwinner was killed or no longer able to hold down a well-paid job.

The Second World War

On 3 September 1939, war was declared, though the country had effectively been on a war footing for months. Petrol was rationed immediately in 1939, but by early 1940 it included bacon, butter and sugar. People were issued with ration books and had to register with a specified shop to get their food. The shopkeeper was only given sufficient food for those who registered at the shop. Almost all foods, were rationed eventually except vegetables, as many could grow them at home. 'Dig for victory' was promoted. Game, such as rabbit, was available and people were able to keep chickens in their gardens. Other food was sold at controlled prices to avoid profiteering.

Clothes went on ration in 1941, with points allocated per item. Ladies' shoes 'cost' seven points or coupons, a dress was eleven points, plus the money cost of the items. The government introduced utility clothing, paring the material used to the minimum. No frills, wide lapels or belts, and shorter skirts. Everyone adopted a make do and mend attitude. Women began to wear slacks (trousers) and siren suits: a boiler suit worn over ordinary clothes to protect them from dirt, especially in an air-raid shelter.

Rationing continued even after the war ended. Bread was rationed in 1946 after a disastrous harvest and potatoes in 1947 because of a severe winter. It was 1954 before all rationing ended.

ARP and fire fighters

The role of the ARP was to organise the public air-raid shelters and check that blackout precautions were being followed. Hazel Wheeler comments that there was quite a lot of 'Fiddling of money – in the blackout one couldn't see fake and foreign coins easily'.[177]

In addition, ARPs had to help in the aftermath of a bombing raid, rescuing people from ruins, giving first aid, recovering bodies. Many people could obtain a private air-raid shelter, known as Anderson shelters, to put in their back garden. Schools had shelters in the playgrounds and many businesses also provided air-raid shelters for their employees.

In October 1940, two high-explosive bombs dropped in the Lindley area, together with almost a hundred incendiary bombs. In December the same year, Wellington Mills was hit by two parachute mines and one high-explosive bomb. Houses were also damaged and windows shattered.

Nellie Paxman joined the fire services and became a sector captain. She took notes on how to deal with incendiaries, organise teams responsible for particular sections, send messengers to other groups to check all incendiaries had been dealt with, check the deployment of staff and dismiss them when the work was over.[178]

In residential areas, up to thirty houses would be 'watched' by each group of twenty to thirty people, under the control of the section captain. Hazel Wheeler described how the headmistress at Greenhead, Miss Annie Hill, and her staff formed a fire-watching rota and slept in the school and considered it was 'so eerie at night'.[179]

WVS (Women's Voluntary Services for Air Raid Precautions)

In 1938, a new national ARP unit, called the Women's Voluntary Services (WVS), was set-up to help local authorities by providing warders, nurses, drivers, clerks, cooks, typists, domestic helpers and waitresses.[180]

The WVS liaised with the local authority and ARP personnel and helped with the domestic aspects of air-raids – evacuating people, producing bandages from old sheets and pillow cases and supplying nightwear. The work expanded to include arranging collections of rose hips (rose hip syrup alleviated colds), providing canteen services at railway stations, or even mobile ones that could be set-up wherever needed, giving talks on domestic issues, such as how to make the most of the food available, and finding temporary accommodation for the homeless. They ran clubs, staffed hostels for women and for soldiers, helped in hospitals and in community kitchens. The name was changed to the Women's Voluntary Service for Civil Defence, but kept the WVS acronym.

Conscription

In 1941, conscription for women began. All women between the ages of 18 and 60 had to register, stating which job they would 'like' to go to. Only single women or childless widows between 20 and 30 were called-up first, but those age limits soon expanded to include 19- to 40-year-olds. Women who had served in the First World War could be conscripted up to the age of 50. In the Second World War, women's jobs expanded to include driving, mechanics and maintenance of army vehicles, flying aircraft from factories to the air bases, manning anti-aircraft guns and breaking German codes.

If women chose not to join any of the armed forces, they could choose munitions work such as building tanks, planes, bombs, guns and any other machinery needed for the war, or go into the Land Army. In 1942, a special employment exchange was set-up in Huddersfield to find part-time work for married women so that they could free-up single women who could then find 'war work'.

Wartime laws

The Emergency Powers (Defence) Act provided for almost any action that could be designated public safety and order.

Mrs Annie Hale from Sheepridge had agreed that she would send her husband a telegram stating that their daughter was seriously ill. This she did and he was granted a week's compassionate leave. She then sent a second telegram, purported to come from their doctor, saying that his wife was dangerously ill. The commanding officer was suspicious and contacted the doctor who denied all knowledge of the telegram. The court fined her £5 to be paid off at 5 shillings (25p) a week. This would have caused her considerable hardship since her income was only 42 shillings (£2.10) and she had five children.[181]

Refugees

During May and June 1940, the Germans overran the Benelux countries, causing a mass exodus, primarily to Britain. Huddersfield began preparations for them as well as preparing for an influx of children from Bradford, who were to be sent to the outlying villages such as Wooldale and Honley. The refugees were to be housed initially in Sunday school buildings, prepared for the occasion, but proper billets were needed. Speakers of French, Flemish and Dutch were also appealed for.

Then Dunkirk happened and the soldiers rescued were distributed across the country, including to Huddersfield, where hundreds were taken to billets throughout the town.

Refugees from the Benelux countries also arrived, consisting mainly of women and young children. By 28 June, refugees from the Channel Islands also came to Huddersfield. These were not the expected unaccompanied children, but whole families who all needed accommodation.

Somehow all these refugees were gradually housed and supported until the end of the war.[182]

Evacuees

Evacuation generally began early in 1939, but by 1941 Huddersfield received notice that it was to be sent 500 children from the south coast. Mrs E. Walker, the new billeting and welfare officer, appealed for billets.[183]

Later in the year, evacuee children began to arrive and were taken to Deanhouse in Holmfirth before being found suitable billets.

Foreign troops

Troops from different nations arrived in Huddersfield, including those from the Baltic countries and prisoners-of-war from Germany and Italy. The ones that caused the most controversy were the Americans, though they didn't come into the war until December 1941. They seemed to be better paid than our own troops and had the advantages of having access to more luxury goods, which were sent to them, as well as being seen as exotic and different.

Volunteer work

The Huddersfield Spitfire Fund had raised £15,858 by October 1941, enough to buy three of the legendary 400mph aircraft, named Huddersfield I, II and III.

The Huddersfield and District Women's Wartime Bureau[184] formed at the beginning of the war was the place to go to when advice was needed. Local regiments, national military and the Red Cross were all supported through fundraising, providing 'comforts' of food packages, presents at Christmas or gifts of clothing. The women organised eighteen working parties to visit the billets of the ATS to contact the girls personally, helped them settle in and gave help if needed. The WVS stored much of their clothing there for distribution in case of blitz bombing in Huddersfield.

Their report for 1944 shows how much effort was put into this organisation, just one of many charities helping the war effort in Huddersfield. Requisitions were regularly received from all the services, often needed urgently. One from the WVS was for a thousand pairs of socks for the Merchant Navy. This was completed within two months. They also had in stock over 3,000 knitted garments awaiting instructions from the national director of voluntary organisations, whose own depot had been blitzed.

Another useful innovation was the Clothing Exchange run by an executive committee. At a time of rationing of material, it was very hard to keep replacing children's clothing, so the exchange arranged for mothers to exchange children's clothing for larger sizes.

The bureau organised a receiving room for items handed in, a packing room and a sewing room, with sewing machines. In the five years of its existence, the women dealt with 35,000 pairs of socks, doled out 45,000lb of wool for knitting, sent 200,000 garments out and made up 12,000 different garments.

Working parties across Huddersfield and district supported the work of the bureau. Almost every church, political party or society of any sort had working parties at which women would sew or knit or raise funds. The Crosland Hill Knitting Circle was one of many set-up to knit anything and everything needed. They held whist drives, raffles, bring and buy, knitting teas and sausage teas as fundraisers. Mrs Kaye held her own birthday knitting party for the cause.

Kath Croft discussed her memories of growing up during the war and its impact on her family:

During the war, my mother knitted – she was part of a Knitting Circle. I remember being trailed off, when I was ill, to sit with them, all these ladies knitting, knitting socks and balaclavas for soldiers.

We had visitors coming one day and Mother got some neck of mutton and some mutton bones. She cooked them and picked all the meat off. Then she let it set and took the fat off the top to make steak pie, using the fat into the flour and the meat she'd scraped, with some vegetables. It was beautiful, she'd made this out of nothing.

We used to go collecting nettles to make nettle beer and blackberries and my father collected mushrooms; his mother was a herbalist so he knew which ones were safe to pick.[185]

Holidays at home[186]

Huddersfield Corporation helped pioneer, from 1941 onwards, the 'Holidays at Home' project. They organised events, suitable for different interests, different ages. In 1943 they produced a booklet, with full details of the activities available during the summer. Events took place in Greenhead Park, the Town Hall and local cinemas.

Nora Bray formed a group called the Follies on Parade, who travelled the north of England entertaining the troops. As the troupe had young girls as well as young women, there was always a matron with them. The Huddersfield Entertainment Committee had two buses, one of which was used to carry the troupe and other entertainers around Huddersfield and the north. The other was converted into a small theatre able to seat up to fourteen people. Nora Bray was the act chosen to help test this theatre on its debut in 1940.

The Ritz cinema, which had opened in 1936, showed films such as *Casablanca*, *Navy Blues* and *Yankee Doodle Dandy*. Dancing was available in the Town Hall and in a marquee in Greenhead Park almost every night. During the day there were Punch and Judy shows, donkey rides, children's roundabouts and paddling pools.

Morality concerns

Concerns about morality centred on the behaviour of women, not men. It was widely believed that moral standards were declining, particularly in towns. To counteract this behaviour, there was an increase in promoting patriotism, in fostering British values. Moral weakness was seen as being unBritish.

Between 1939 and 1941, the number of new cases of venereal disease reported almost doubled. In 1942 the numbers rose even more sharply after the arrival of American troops. One suggestion was to relax the ban on advertising these facts and on solutions to them. The newspapers and radio began to publicise what was happening, explaining both the causes and the remedies. There was an emphasis on education to reduce incidents of venereal disease. Both the army and civilian sexual health agencies had learned from their experiences during the First World War, and were better prepared for the Second

World War. Fortunately, the discovery of penicillin provided a medical solution.

After the war

Victory in Europe (VE) celebrations took place all over Huddersfield and festivities in Greenhead Park. According to Hazel Wheeler, Mary Brown of Edgerton gave £5 for every baby born on VE day and VE day plus one, who survived one month. The money had to go into a Post Office savings bank.[187]

Britain was badly affected financially during the war, as well as having to repair the considerable infrastructural damage from bombing. The General Election in 1945 brought in a Labour government committed to very expensive social reforms and nationalisation of major industries. The huge war loans from America had to be repaid.

There was an acute housing shortage so prefabs (prefabricated homes) intended to last about five to ten years were built. The first ones in this area were built in Dalton with others at Netheroyd Hill. During the winter of 1946/47, water running down the inside walls during the day froze at night, producing icicles of up to 6 feet (2 metres) in length.[188]

Television and radio broadcasts were curtailed, newspapers and magazines restricted. Blackouts became a regular feature of life. There were food shortages because crops froze in the ground and potatoes were rationed for the first time. Factories were forced to shut so more people had to claim unemployment benefit. Once the snow thawed, there was major flooding and the Wharfe, Derwent, Aire and Ouse all burst their banks.

The National Health Service was introduced, despite considerable disquiet among doctors and nurses who initially voted against the idea. Taxes were increased to pay for all this and the British economy stagnated.

Many Huddersfield people went on to marry refugees from other countries or became one of the thousands of war brides who set off in 1946 to go to America or Canada.

War brides included foreign women who arrived, mostly from the continent, after marrying English soldiers. The 'Lonely

Brides in Huddersfield' initiative was set-up for girls who found themselves in this situation. They were invited to send their name and address to the Citizen's Advice Bureau (CAB), who could put them in touch with others. Mrs Middlebrook Haigh established it for 'strangers in a strange land, who speak very little English, know very few people and time hangs heavily on their hands'. The CAB had already been successful with one Dutch girl for whom they had found some Dutch novels and provided an English/Dutch dictionary. They were also in touch with several Italian brides and a number of Belgian girls.[189]

CHAPTER NINE

A Moving Population

Emigration

In the second half of the nineteenth century there were gold and diamond discoveries in America, Australia, Canada and South Africa that pulled people away from their homeland. Initially, men often went with their families following later, or young adults went in the hope of finding work. Economic depression in England pushed the unemployed to emigrate. Wars or political upheaval brought refugees from Europe. Some moved on to other countries, some remained in England.

Furness and Mary Longbottom, living in Lockwood in 1891, had spent many years abroad. They'd gone out to Australia around 1855 and had six children who were all born in Victoria. They stayed there for the next twenty-three years before returning to Huddersfield. Their youngest daughter, Agnes, was born on a 'British ship' on the voyage home.

Emigration by women was encouraged because as census statistics became more informative it was realised that there were far more women in Britain than men, even before two world wars decimated the male population. In the colonies, it was the reverse. Men vastly outnumbered women. Women could not emigrate as easily as men, primarily because they lacked the capital to do so. Very poor women could claim help from the Poor Law guardians, but what the newly emerging countries wanted were educated, hard-working women, who would contribute more to their society. It was this situation that many emigration societies sought to remedy.

Some occupations were not required. Mantle-makers and needlewomen generally would find little work for them in Australia, leading them to either starve or be 'driven into evil courses'.[190]

Newspaper advertisements during the 1850s concentrated primarily on voyages to Australia, but by the 1880s this changed to reflect the demand for passage to the Americas. Agencies had opened in Huddersfield for shipping leaving Liverpool. Free land grants of 160 acres could be obtained in Canada, which would be a big incentive to many agricultural labourers and small farmers.

As well as emigrating permanently, many emigrated then returned. Harriet Ledger was born in Huddersfield in 1844. She married Hiram Noble in 1864 and they emigrated to America in 1870, working in a woollen mill in Massachusetts.[191] Their eldest son, Fred, was born there. Around 1875, they returned to England, living in Lindley, where sons Josh and Thomas were born. By 1881, Harriet was a widow with three small children. She became a worsted-mender and returned to live with her father, Thomas. In 1891, her occupation was woollen burler, but in 1901 Harriet was the head of household. Living with her were son Thomas, a woollen piece scourer, and her sister Emma Ledger, a woollen feeder. Harriet died in 1912.

Tom Graham was a dyer but the whole family went with him when he went to Germany. His daughter Milly was born in Grumberg and his son Oscar in Berlin. By 1891 they were back in England, living in Longwood.

This willingness to move for job opportunities gave the women a chance to live abroad and experience a different way of life because of their husbands' jobs at a time when it was difficult for women to migrate on their own.

Immigration

Just as many people left England, many arrived, sometimes in small numbers coming primarily because of a specific occupation, sometimes in large numbers because of catastrophes in their homeland. There were strong links between textile firms in Huddersfield and those in Germany. Two members of the Lowenthal family came to Huddersfield in the 1850s. Louis (or Lewis) was already married to Ida and they had three children when they arrived. Ten years later, they had a fourth child, Ellen, born in Huddersfield. By then his brother Joseph had married a German lady, Bertha, but their four children were all born in Huddersfield. Their daughter, also Bertha, went on to become a staunch supporter of the WSPU during its suffrage campaigns and all the family were involved in a variety of philanthropic ventures in the area.

Irish

The largest influx of Irish came after the potato famine of the 1840s, when the potato crop failed. In 1847, Huddersfield was organising a meeting in the Philosophical Hall to raise funds for 'the appalling destitution which prevails in Ireland'.[192]

Apart from general labouring, the Irish were often hawkers of various commodities, such as the Devaney family who lived in Kirkburton in 1851. Biddy was a hawker of pots, as was one of her sons. Another was a coalminer, but the rest of the family were all hawkers of oranges. Many Irish became servants like Catherine Colburt aged 17, a kitchen maid, and Kate Mahoney aged 50, an upper nurse, who in 1861 were both employed in the household of Bentley Shaw, JP.

The Irish tended to live in very poor lodgings under the worst possible conditions. Eventually, all lodging-house-keepers had to have a licence or face prosecution. Twenty-three people, principally Irish, were summoned, mainly from Castlegate, Post Office Yard, Manchester Street and Upperhead Row for this reason.[193]

Not everyone who came from Ireland was a destitute pauper. At Samuel Ball's private school on Fitzwilliam Street, he employed two ladies from Ireland: Eleanor Gison, who was a teacher/governess, and Emily Gison, who was a music teacher, both from Derry. The Leblans family lived in Ramsden Street.

John was a professor of physics and his wife was a schoolteacher, both from Ireland. Harriett Cheveley from Ireland was the principal of Huddersfield Girls' School for the whole of its independent existence.

By the end of the nineteenth century, the Irish as a group had largely been absorbed into the rest of the community. As wages increased, the families spread out into other areas. The principal point of cohesion was through their religion, as most were Catholics. St Patrick's Catholic Church was built in 1832 at the instigation of the Catholic community in Huddersfield. The church set-up Sunday schools for both adults and children, as well as supporting education for the wider community. Later, St Patrick's Church School provided general education for Catholic children in the area and was monitored, like the board schools, by the Huddersfield School Board.

Jews

One of the problems in finding out about Jewish women's experiences is that they are rarely mentioned in newspapers. The women were more likely to stay at home to look after the family or work within the home or family business. Their input is often by implication.

The Fisherson family appear in Huddersfield in 1891, when Hyman Fisherson set-up a business in Robinsons Yard, Bradford Road. He was a tailor from Russia, his wife Matilda a tailoress from Poland. They had two children, both born in Leeds. Living with them was Hyman's sister Sophia, a buttonholer. They also had a number of lodgers, all male, all from Poland or Russia and all working in the tailoring business. It is probable that they were Jews but the census does not give specific information.

Not all came as impoverished refugees. The Zossenheim family were definitely of the wealthy middle-class. Max Zossenheim married Rachel Frances Moses in London in 1862. Their eldest daughter was born in Paris a year later, but they came to Huddersfield shortly after this. All their next four children were born in Huddersfield, where they lived in Clyde

House, Edgerton. Max was a manufacturer and merchant who eventually took English nationality. They stayed for twenty years before moving to Leeds.

Once the male head of household became a British citizen, this applied to all the family, including his wife. Many Jews changed their names to become more anglicised. Solomon Shoolberg had a wallpaper shop in Huddersfield at the beginning of the twentieth century. In 1917, like many others with German names, he changed his family's surname to a more English name, taking the name of Schofield.

No synagogue has ever been built in Huddersfield, nor is there a Jewish cemetery but in the 1900s, rooms in Northumberland Street were used for services. Rooms in Albion Street were used as a synagogue in the 1940s. The congregation set-up contact groups for Jewish soldiers and refugees in Huddersfield and surrounding areas. The Albion Street synagogue closed in the 1960s due to a fall in congregation. The total Jewish population never seems to have risen above eighty or ninety people.

Polish

Polish refugees came during and after the Second World War. Some because they hoped for a better economic life, but like many others, Maria Borsukiewicz came because 'we were frightened to go back to Poland' after the war. 'We decided to come to England,' she said.[194]

As Catholics, the Polish people found support from the Irish Catholic community, who allowed them to use St Patrick's Church for their own services. In 1948, the Polish White Cross Society was established. Among other activities, they offered Polish classes specifically aimed at helping English women who were marrying Polish men and needed to learn the language.

Other refugees came from the Ukraine, Latvia and Czechoslovakia. A Refugee Club was formed in 1939, providing support for those from eastern Europe. By 1943, there were sufficient numbers for each nation to form their own clubs, such as the Czechoslovak Friendship Club in Westgate. The

Huddersfield branch of the Association of Ukrainians in Great Britain was formed in 1947 and eventually opened its own Ukrainian club in Edgerton. In 1948, a group of fifty 'European Voluntary Workers' (EVW) arrived in Huddersfield. The EVW was a scheme to offer work to displaced persons, while helping the shortage of labour in Britain. Middlemost & Co arranged accommodation for the workers and their families. Some of the workers had not had a settled home for the previous six or seven years, but came and learnt weaving and mending.[195]

Commonwealth countries

In 1948, HMT *Empire Windrush* docked at Tilbury. On board were migrants from the Caribbean. Though some intended staying only a few years, many settled in Britain and at least eight of them came to Huddersfield. There is now a large Afro-Caribbean community in Huddersfield, which annually celebrates with a colourful carnival.

The equally large Asian community, of people from India, Pakistan and Bangladesh, did not really develop until the late 1950s and 1960s, when many came to work in the textile industry.

Bibliography

Challenge and Change: A Brief History of Women Councillors in Yorkshire & the Humber (Centre for Women & Democracy, 2011)

The Huddersfield Glee and Madrigal Society: A Jubilee Record (1926)

Huddersfield Holidays at Home: Souvenir Booklet (1943)

Balmforth, Owen, *The Huddersfield Industrial Society* (1910)

Baren, Maurice, *Victorian Shopping* (Michael O'Mara Books Ltd, 1998)

Barnes, C., *Disabled People in Britain: a case for anti-discrimination legislation* (C. Hurst & Co, 1991)

Beddoe, Deirdre, *Back to Home and Duty* (Pandora, 1989)

Bradley, Simon, *The Railways: Nation, Network & People* (Profile Books Ltd, 2015)

Burnett, J., *England eats out: a social history of eating out in England from 1830 to the present* (Routledge, 2004)

Burton, Alan, *The British Consumer Co-operative Movement and Film* (Manchester University Press, 2005)

D'Cruze, Shani, ed., *Everyday Violence in Britain, 1850-1950* (Pearson Education Ltd, 2000)

Duncan, Isabelle, *Skirting the Boundary: A history of women's cricket* (The Robson Press, 2013)

Frye, Kate, *Campaigning for the Vote, a post-1911 diary* (Francis Boutle, Post 1911)

Gourvish, TR & O'Day, A., ed., *Later Victorian Britain 1867-1900* (MacMillan Education, 1988)

Haigh, H., ed., *Huddersfield: a most handsome town* (Kirklees Cultural Services, 1992)

Harrison, J.F.C., *Late Victorian Britain 1875-1901* (Fontana Press, 1990)

Harley, M. & Ingilby, J., *Life and Tradition in West Yorkshire* (Smith Settle Ltd, 1990)

Hey, David, *How our Ancestors Lived* (Public Record Office, 2002)

Horn, Pamela, *The Rise and Fall of the Victorian Servant* (Sutton Publishing Ltd, 1995)

Hunt, C.J., *Sex Versus Class in Two British Trade Unions in the Early Twentieth Century (Journal of Women's History,* volume 24(1):84-110, 2012*)*

Hunt, Cathy, *The National Federation of Women Workers, 1906-1921* (Palgrave MacMillan, 2014)

Jackson, Alan A., *The Middle Classes 1900-1950* (David St John Thomas, 1991)

Lang, C., *Keep smiling through: women in the Second World War,* (Cambridge University Press, 1989)

Laybourn K., *Unemployment & Employment Policies concerning women in Britain 1900-1951* (Edwin Mellen Press Ltd, 1992)

Levine, Philippa, *Victorian Feminism 1850-1900* (Century Hutchinson Ltd, 1987)

Liddington, J., *Rebel Girls: Their fight for the vote* (Virago Press, 2008)

Littlewood, Ann, *Storthes Hall Remembered* (University of Huddersfield, 2003)

Lowe, Graham, *Women in the administrative revolution: the feminization of clerical work* (Univesity of Toronto, 1987)

Marland, H., *Medicine and Society in Wakefield and Huddersfield 1780-1870* (Cambridge University Press, 1987)

Mayo, C.M., *Co-operative House-building* (Women's Co-operative Guild, 1898)

Minter, G. & E., *Discovering Old Huddersfield Pt1-5* (1993)

Newby, J., *Women's Lives* (Pen & Sword Books Ltd, 2011)

Nicholson, Virginia, *Singled Out* (Viking Books Ltd, 2007)

Parr, Linda Jean, *The history of libraries in Halifax and Huddersfield from the sixteenth century to the coming of the public libraries* (PHD Thesis, University of London, 2003)

Perks, R.B., *The New Liberalism and the Challenge of Labour in the W R of Yorkshire 1885-1914* (Thesis University of Huddersfield eprint, 1985)

Phillips, C., *The Impact of the First World War upon the status and employment of women with reference to Huddersfield* (Dissertation, Huddersfield University, 1995)

Roberts, Elizabeth, *Women's Work 1840-1940* (Economic History Society, 1988)

Rose, S.O., Sex, Citizenship and the Nation in WW2 Britain, in *The American Historical Review*, Volume 103, Issue 4, 1 October 1998 (American Historical Review, 1998)

Rushworth, G., *Rushworth's Ltd of Huddersfield, the Story of a Department Store* (J.D.M. & G. Rushworth, 1999)

Seddon, L., *British Women Composers* (Routledge, 2013)

Sharples, E. (née Hoyle), *My Life's Work* (unpublished manuscript, Bury Central Library, 1968)

Sheard, N. et al, *A Short History of Messrs Armitage, Sykes & Hinchcliffe* (Private publication)

Smith, H.L., *The British women's suffrage campaign 1866-1928* (Routledge, 1998)

Tate, Tim, *Girls with Balls: The Secret History of Women's Football* (John Blake Publishing Ltd, 2013)

Teasdale, V., *Foul Deeds and Suspicious Deaths around Huddersfield* (Pen & Sword Books Ltd, 2007)

Teasdale, V., *Mill Memories* (Pen & Sword Books Ltd, 2006)

Teasdale, V., *Huddersfield in the Great War* (Pen & Sword Books Ltd, 2014)

Vicinus, Martha, ed., *Suffer and be Still: Women in the Victorian Age* (Indiana University Press, 1972)

Walvin, James, *Victorian Values* (Andre Deutsch Ltd, 1987)

Wearing, J.P., *The London Stage 1900-1909: A Calendar of Productions, Performers, and Personnel* (Scarecrow Press, 2014)

Wheeler, Hazel, *Huddersfield at War* (Alan Sutton Publishing, 1992)

Wheeler, Hazel, *Living on Tick* (Alan Sutton Publishing, 2009)

Wheeler, Hazel, *Sing a Song of Sixpence* (Alan Sutton Publishing, 1995)

Wightman, Clare, *More than Munitions: women, work and the engineering industries 1900-1950* (Addison Wesley Longman Publications, 1999)

William, J., *A Game for Rough Girls* (Routledge, 2003)

Williams, J., *Cricket & England* (Frank Class, 2003)

Wilmhurst, W.L., *The Huddersfield Choral Society 1836-1961* (Booklet)

Women's Co-operative Guild, *Maternity: Letters from Working Women* (G. Bell & Sons Ltd, 1915)

Yeo, Stephen, ed., *Routledge Revivals: New Views of Co-operation (1988)* (Routledge, 1988)

Miscellaneous Sources

http://www.redcross.org.uk/About-us/Who-we-are/History-and-origin/First-World-War

https://huddersfield.exposed

http://www.nationalarchives.gov.uk/humanrights/1848-1914/
http://www.donmouth.co.uk/womens_football/huddersfield_atalanta.html
Census Returns 1851-1911
Birth, Marriage and Death Indexes 1837-1950
Huddersfield Daily Examiner Trinity Mirror Group
Huddersfield Chronicle & West Yorkshire Advertiser
British Journal of Nursing MA Healthcare Ltd

Endnotes

Abbreviations

HC = The *Huddersfield Chronicle* and *West Yorkshire Advertiser*
HE = *Huddersfield Daily Examiner*
YEP = *Yorkshire Evening Post*
LM = *Leeds Mercury*
LT = *Leeds Times*

Endnotes

1. HC 12 January 1867
2. HC 18 February 1871
3. C85/3/6/14/p103/1 Reports from Stanley Royd
4. LT 11 December 1858
5. HC July-October 1900
6. HC 27 December 1873
7. HC 21 July 1860
8. Co-operative Women's Guild, *Maternity: letters from working women* 1915
9. HC 17 March 1894
10. HE 8 January 1948
11. E Chilvers, family history notes
12. Mrs Beeton's *Book of Household Management 1899*
13. HC 10 July 1855
14. Mrs Beeton's *Book of Household Management 1899*
15. HC 3 January 1880
16. Mrs Beeton's *Book of Household Management 1899*
17. K Croft, family history notes
18. N Sheard, *A Short History of Messrs Armitage, Sykes & Hinchcliffe*
19. HC 3 September 1887
20. E Chilvers, family history notes
21. Shelia Dixon, family history notes
22. HC 21 October 1876
23. HC 19 October 1872
24. HC 8 December 1879
25. FEI/1/1-3 Minute books of the Female Education Institute

26 HC 1 January 1877
27 HC 23 October 1858
28 FEI/1/1-3 1859 *Minute Books of Female Education Institution*
29 KC314/2/4 Huddersfield Girls' College minutes, 1871-79
30 HC 29 July 1893
31 HE 1 July 1936
32 HC 18 May 1850
33 HC 1 September 1877
34 HC 11 January 1873
35 S/HOH/1 KCZ0030/1-2 *Orphanages Minute book and attendance register*
36 HE 25 March 1941
37 John Taylor *Epidemic Cholera in Huddersfield and the Neighbourhood* 1849
38 HE 22 to 23 April 1913
39 HE 30 November 1905
40 KC981/2/1 *Memoirs of E M Harling*
41 KC853/1-3 *Newspaper Cuttings Nurse Dorothy Wood*
42 LM 2 July 1831
43 HC 20 April 1889
44 *British Journal of Nursing* June 1933
45 HC 22 August 1883
46 HC 9 June 1885
47 HC 9 June 1886
48 HE 1 June 1948
49 HC 30 June 1890
50 C85/3/6/14/p103/1 *Reports from Stanley Royd*
51 Ann Littlewood, *Storthes Hall Remembered*, 2003
52 HC 28 March 1896
53 HC 16 September 1892
54 HE 28 July 1936
55 HE 18 June 1938
56 HC 19 April 1873
57 HC 17 July 1880
58 HE 10 June 1931
59 HE 7 November 1945
60 Owen Balmforth *The Huddersfield Industrial Society* 1910
61 G Rushworth *Rushworth's Ltd of Huddersfield, the Story of a Department Store* 1999
62 HE 23 April 1913
63 N Sheard, *A Short History of Messrs Armitage, Sykes & Hinchcliffe*
64 HE 9 May 1927

ENDNOTES

65 HE 14 February 1949
66 Simon Bradley, *The Railways: Nation, Network & People, 2004*
67 HC 24 December 1859
68 R B Perks, *The New Liberalism and the Challenge of Labour in the W R of Yorkshire 1885-1914,* 1985
69 HE 18 June 1948
70 HC 6 April 1891
71 *Nottingham Evening Post*, 21 November 1906
72 HE 28 July 1913
73 HE 19 December 1906
74 KC1060/1 Minutes of WSPU, Huddersfield branch
75 *The Times*, March 28 1907
76 Archives Co-op Guild
77 Owen Balmforth *The Huddersfield Industrial Society,* 1910
78 C. M. Mayo, *Co-operative House-building* , 1898
79 HC 9 February 1883
80 HC 23 November 1883
81 HC 23 November 1883
82 HC 19 June and 24 July 1852
83 HC 12 July 1873
84 HC 13 June 1868
85 HC 2 June 1855
86 HC April to June 1851-1881
87 HC 7 November 1895
88 HE 17 February 1936
89 HC 12 October 1896
90 N/QS/RMT/1 *The Rock Mission, Turnbridge*
91 HC 18 January 1890
92 C118 Wakefield prison records
93 H 18 May 1850
94 HC 25 September 1880
95 HC 30 June 1855
96 HE 27 July 1938
97 HC 18 December 1852
98 HC 20 February 1858
99 HC 1 March 1890
100 HC 23 June 1893
101 HE 16 March 1949
102 HC 9 May 1863
103 HC April/August 1869
104 HC 29 December 1894
105 HC 26 August 1899

106 Sharples, E nee Hoyle *My Life's Work,* 1968
107 WYP/HU/A147/1-13 Lily M Allen
108 HE 7 February 1949
109 N Sheard, *A Short History of Messrs Armitage, Sykes & Hinchcliffe*
110 HE 28 November 1945
111 HE 12 June 1913
112 HE 8 June 1948
113 HE 24 March 1949
114 HE 29 July 1946
115 HC 21 January 1854
116 HC 1 April 1880
117 HC 28 September 1880
118 G Rushworth *Rushworth's Ltd of Huddersfield, the Story of a Department Store* 1999
119 HC 20 December 1890
120 HC 13 December 1894
121 HC 29 December 1900
122 HE 14 February 1936
123 HE 13 June 1941
124 HE 3 January 1948
125 HC 1 February 1873
126 HC 31 December 1890
127 W L Wilmhurst *The Huddersfield Choral Society 1836-1961*
128 HC 4 June 1864
129 HC 4 June 1864
130 HC 11 October 1856
131 HC 20 December 1856
132 HC 4 June 1864
133 HC 25 May 1888
134 *The Times* 25 November 1916
135 HE 7 March 1917
136 HE 28 March 1949
137 KC508 Frances Mary Hefford Cocking
138 HE 16 and 18 April 1945
139 *Holmfirth Express* 9 June 1928
140 *Holmfirth Express* 30 June 1928
141 *Holmfirth Express* July-August 1928
142 HE 25 June 1930
143 HE 1 May 1933
144 *Hampshire Telegraph and Sussex Chronicle 26* January 1895
145 HE 6 February 1929
146 *Bath Chronicle* 12 March 1921

147 www.donmouth.co.uk
148 HE 18 January 1922
149 *Hull Daily Mail* 8 February 1922
150 HC 17 February 1898
151 *Manchester Times* 19 October 1861
152 LT 23 April 1887
153 HC 26 August and 30 December 1890
154 LT 25 October 1845
155 HC 16 February 1898
156 HC 11 January 1916
157 LM 27 February 1875
158 HC 16 March 1887
159 HC 13 January 1890
160 HE 13 July 1931
161 HC 4 April 1893
162 Sheila Dixon, family history notes
163 HD 2 June 1948
164 HC 31 May 1900
165 HC 18 December 1900
166 V Teasdale *Huddersfield at War*, 2014
167 Ibid
168 HE 24 July 1916
169 HE 17 January 1918
170 HE 3 April 1917
171 Sharples, E nee Hoyle *My Life's Work*, 1968
172 HE 20 May 1917
173 HE 18 March 1918
174 HE 9 October 1918
175 HE 28 July 1915
176 HE 7 December 1915
177 Hazel Wheeler, *Huddersfield at War* 1992
178 KC282/1 & 2 & /3 Nellie Paxman notes
179 Hazel Wheeler, *Huddersfield at War* 1992
180 HE 16 June 1938
181 HE 12 June 1940
182 HE May-June 1940
183 HE 14 March 1941
184 KC61/4 Huddersfield Women's Wartime Bureau
185 K Croft, family history
186 *Huddersfield Holidays at Home* 1943
187 Hazel Wheeler, *Huddersfield at War*, 1992
188 HE 17 February 1947

189 HE 11 July 1946
190 HC 5 April 1893
191 US Census, 1870
192 HC 23 January 1847
193 HC 10 August 1850
194 V Teasdale *Huddersfield Mill Memories,* 2006
195 HE 8 January 1948

Index

Abram, Miss M. A., 42
Allen, Lily Mary, 88
Armitage, Hannah, 83

Baines, Mrs, 38
Bake, Mrs, 85
Balmforth, Amy, 57
Bannister, Mrs, 38
Bardsley, Mrs, 44
Barraclough, Mrs, 108
Barraclough, Mrs L., 107
Barry, Miss Emily, 42
Bates, Miss Edith, 59
Battye, Miss Mabel, 59
Bayldon, Widow, 92
Beanland, Elsie, 102
Beaumont, Ann, 53
Beaumont, Charlotte Elizabeth
  see Beaumont, Lottie, 101
Beaumont, Letitia, 113
Beaumont, Lottie, 99, 102
Beaumont, Mrs, 51–2, 76
Beaumont, Sarah Ann, 76
Beddows, Miss, 22
Bedford, Nancy, 5
Beeton, Mrs, 10, 12, 110, 154
Beever, Ellen, 68
Berry, Martha, 92
Beverley, Phyllis, 89
Bickerstaff, Mary, 36
Blackburn, Martha, 48

Blamires, Mary, 1, 38, 64, 118
Booth, Catherine, 77
Booth, Eliza, 30
Booth, Miss, 22
Borsukiewicz, Maria, 137
Bottomley, Eleanor, 93
Bottomley, Nanny
  see Rhodes, Nanny, 54
Bottomley, Sarah, 53
Bowker, Ellen, 92
Boyd, Dr Catherine Laura, 39
Boyle, Miss Winifred, 112
Bray, Mrs, 75
Bray, Nora, 130
Briggs, Mary, 33
Broadbent, Miss, 38
Broadbent, Mrs Betty, 117
Broadbent, née Crabtree, Ellen (Helen), 55
Broadbent, Nellie, 121
Broadbent, Violet, 113
Broadhead, Miss, 107
Brook, Mary Ann, 5
Brook, Miss, 20, 22
Brooke, Ellen, 68
Brown, Mary, 131
Burton, Alice, 92
Burton, Mrs, 92
Byrne, Miss, 23

Carter, Miss, 22
Cartwright, Doreen, 89

Casey, Winifred, 81
Cheveley, Miss Harriett M., 27, 136
Chilvers, Eileen, iv
Clare, Miss, 21
Clarke, Hilda, 107
Clarkson, Mrs, 90
Clasby, Mary, 81
Cocking, Frances Mary Hefford, 102
Colburt, Catherine, 135
Cooper, Miss, 22
Croft, Kath, iv, 129, 154
Crosland, Miss, 99
Crummock, Mrs, 76
Cummins, Mrs, 23

D'Arcy, Mrs, 76
Dearnley, Margaret, 8
Demetriadi, Mrs, 38
Devaney, Biddy, 135
Devine, Miss, 44
Dixon, Sheila, iv, 21, 115, 154
Donkersley, Lydia, 66
Donkersley, Mrs, 38
Drake, Mary, 26
Drury, Miss, 23
Duckham, May, 6
Dunch, Ada, 103
Dunn, Ann, 53
Dyer, Mary Ann, 81
Dyson, Mary Ellen, 30
Dyson, Mrs Edgar, 38
Dyson, Mrs F.L., 72

Easingwood, Isabella, 91
Edgely, Miss, 107

England, Florence, 86
England, Madam, 99

Faulder, Nurse Evelyn, 118
Field, Ann, 23
Fielding, Miss Mildred, 60
Firth, Alice, 6
Fisher, Mrs John, 38
Fisherson, Matilda, 136
Ford, Emma, 5
Fountain, Maria, 83
Freeman, Miss, 101
Freeman, Norah, 64
Frobisher, Ada Ann, 17

Gaffikin, Dr Prudence Elizabeth, 39
Gardiner, Alice, 64
Gaunt, Mrs, 22
Gilliard, Miss, 22
Gison, Eleanor, 135
Gison, Emily, 135
Glaisyer, Mrs Julia, 64, 90
Gledhill, Priscilla, 33
Goldthorp, Fanny, 26
Goostray, Mary Ann, 30
Graham, Milly, 134
Grant, Mary Ann, 36
Greenwood, Louisa, 78

Haggis, Azubah, 30
Haigh, Dorothy, 89
Haigh, Mary, 8
Haigh, Sarah, 51
Hale, Mrs Annie, 126
Hanson, Mary, 55
Hardwick, Matilda, 32

INDEX 153

Harling, Elsie May, née Hallas, 40
Healey, Alice, 44
Hellewell, Lily, 68
Hellowell Carter, Mary, 55
Hill, Miss, 21
Hill, Miss L., 106
Hinchliffe, Mary Ellen (née Dyson), 30
Hinchliffe, Miss B.M., 59
Hirst, Miss M. M., 36
Hirst, Mrs, 92
Hirst, Mrs Henry, 57, 72
Hobhouse, Emily, 116
Hodgson, Hannah, 51
Holmes, Miss, 23
Honeyball, Miss Nettie, 106
Horn, Mrs, 117
Horton, Miss, 22
Hoyle, Edith, 88, 120
Hoyle, Lilian, 30
Hoyle, Mary Ann, 88
Humphries, Miss R.W., 106
Huth, Mrs, 45
Huth, Mrs Frank see Moore, Bertha, 114

Imrie, Elizabeth, 78
Irving, Mary, 38
Irving, Miss Mary, 90, 122

Jackson, Alice, 86
Jessop, Gertrude, 64
Jessop, Miss, 20
Jowett, Betty, 33
Jowett, Sarah, 88

Kaley, Mrs Annie, 76
Kay, Mrs Irving, 99
Kaye, Ann, 85
Kaye, Caroline, 51
Kaye, Mrs, 129
Kaye, Mrs W.J., 45
Kelly, Miss, 22
Kelway, Phyllis, 103
Kendall, Mary, 92
Kenworthy, Minnie, 107
Kenworthy, Mrs, 34
Key, Edith, 67–9
Kilner Clarke, Mrs, 65, 119
King, Ada, 121
King, Janet, 64
Kippas, Hannah, 29
Kirby, Mrs Elizabeth, 53
Kitson, Hannah, 30

Ledger, Emma, 134
Lee, Ethel, 107
Lee, Miss Molly, 60
Livingstone, Miss, 23
Longbottom, Mary, 133
Lowenthal, Ellen, 135
Lowenthal, Ida, 135
Lowenthal, Miss, 45

Mahoney, Kate, 135
Mallinson, Miss, 45
Mann, Gladys, 113
Marshall, Mrs A., 94
Marshall, Mrs A.B., 12
Marshall, Mrs Ann, 53
Marshall, Mrs Mary K., 57
Mary, Princess, 43
Mayo, Miss C.M., 72

McGrath, Harriet, 33
Meller, Elizabeth, 33
Mellor, Eliza, 36
Mellor, Mrs, 79
Mellor, Susan, 92
Merrifield, Mrs, 57
Micklethwaite, Hannah, 38
Middlebrook Haigh, Mrs, 132
Millbank, Miss, 80
Milnes, Miss A., 98
Mitchell, Lily, 107
Mitchell, Miss, 108
Montgomery, Kate, 113
Moore, Bertha, 113
Moore, Miss Elsie, 60
Moseley, Lydia, 53
Mosely, Sarah Jane, 99
Murray, Jessie, 40

Nichol, Miss Doris, 59
Noble, Harriet (née Ledger), 134

Pankhurst, Christobel, 67
Pankhurst, Emmeline, 67
Pankhurst, Sylvia, 67
Parbrook, Dr Margaret, 87
Parker, Annie, 44
Parker, Mrs, 76
Patten, Marguerite, 12
Paxman, Nellie, 125
Peace, Mrs James, 98
Peace, Mrs Lister, 98
Pearson, Miss Dorothy, 60
Pinnance, Elizabeth, 68
Pitkethly, Mrs, 26
Platts, Mrs C.W., 66

Pogson, Nellie, 87
Pogson, Sarah, 68
Pyrah, Matilda, 38
Pyrah, Matilda, née Faux, 37

Radcliffe, Miss, 92
Radcliffe, Sarah, 74
Ramsden, Miss Mary, 76
Ratcliffe, Sarah, 7
Renshaw, Mrs, 88
Rhodes, Mrs, 38
Rhodes, Nanny, 54
Roberts, Mrs, 38
Roberts, Mrs Alfred, 38
Roberts, Mrs J. M., 38
Robinson, Mrs, 79
Robson, Mrs Joshua, 77
Rodgers, Miss, 73
Roebuck, Louisa, 33
Rothwell, Mrs, 53
Rowbottom, Mrs Harry, 19
Rowley, Mrs, 88
Rowley, Pattie, 111

Sanderson, Mrs Mary, 76
Saunders, Harriet, 13
Scott, Miss, 106
Scott, Mrs, 45
Senior, Emma, 3
Shaw, Mary, 88
Shaw, Miss Marjorie, 60
Shaw, Mrs Alfred, 57
Sheard, Mrs, 117
Shepherd, Elizabeth, 20
Shepherd, Emily, 20
Shinton, Miss Ethel, 61
Shires, Mrs T., 38

Siddon, Emily, 1, 38, 45, 66, 90
Sidebottom, Mrs T.W., 94
Singleton, Lydia, 3
Singleton, Sarah, 16
Smith, M. A., 28
Smith, Miss J., 22
Staley, Edith, 120
Stanley, Alice, 107
Stanley, Sister Ada, 117
Steele, Miss, 107
Stephens, Miss H., 22
Stopes, Marie, 9
Stott, Selina, 34
Street, Mrs, 76
Strickland, Nurse Jeannie, 118
Studdard, Ellen (Helen), 66
Studdard, Mrs, 38
Summerbill, Miss, 23
Sumner, Mary, 71
Sunderland, Mrs Susan, 99–101, 111
Swift, Hannah, 92
Sykes, Annie, 68
Sykes, Charlotte, 56
Sykes, Elizabeth, 8
Sykes, Mary, 1, 65, 89, 103
Sykes, Miss, 57, 98
Sykes, Mrs C. F., 38
Sykes, Susan
   see Sunderland, Mrs Susan, 99

Tagg, Hilda, 89
Taylor, Miss Marion, 60
Taylor, Mrs, 76

Taylor, Sister Eliza, 75
Thewlis, Dora, 68
Thewlis, Eliza, 68
Thirkill, Miss, 79
Thomson, Doris Scott, 119
Tinker, Miss, 104
Tomlinson, Mrs, 44
Tomlinson, Mrs G.W., 45
Tonnelier, Madame, 20

Varey, Elizabeth, 30

Walker, Frances Sophia, 48
Walker, Honora, 112
Walker, Jane, 46
Walker, Mrs E., 127
Wallace, Naomi, 90
Waller, Constance M., 106–107
Walsh, Bridget, 33
Ward, Mrs Annie, 76
Warren, Eliza, 110
Wheeler, Hazel, 103, 131
Whitham, Miss, 101
Whitman, Mrs W.J., 45
Whitwam, Miss, 108
Whitworth, Ann, 29
Wibberley, Mary A., 113
Wilcox, Miss, 22
Wilkinson, Constance, 102
Wilkinson, Henrietta, 33
Wilkinson, Rhoda, 107
Williamson, Eliza, 44
Wilson, Hypathia, 53
Wilson, Jessica, 53
Wilson, Miss A., 22
Wilson, Miss L., 22

Wood, Annie, 98
Wood, Dorothy, 41
Wood, Georgiana, 54
Wood, Mary, 26

Zossenheim, Rachel Frances
   (née Moses), 136